THE FUTURE OF MANKIND
Affluence Without Wisdom Is Self-Destructive

THE FUTURE OF MANKIND

Affluence
without
WISDOM
is
Self-Destructive

— Second Edition —

TARA SINGH

Life Action Press
Los Angeles, CA

The first edition of *The Future Of Mankind,* published by the Foundation for Life Action in 1986, had the subtitle, *The Branching Of The Road,* and included Chapters 8 through 12 of this revised edition. Portions of Chapters 1 through 4 were included in Tara Singh's *From The City To The Vedic Age Of Shining Beings Extending The Will Of God* published by the Foundation for Life Action in 1983.

Library of Congress Cataloging in Publication Data
Singh, Tara, 1919-
The future of mankind
– affluence without wisdom is self-destructive.
1. Civilization, Modern-1950-
2. Conduct of life. I.Title.
ISBN 1-55531-010-9 Hardbound
ISBN 1-55531-260-8 Softcover

The material from *A Course In Miracles* is used by permission of the copyright owner, the Foundation for Inner Peace, P.O. Box 1104, Glen Ellen, California 95442.

Quotations from *The Grunch Of Giants,* © 1983 by R. Buckminster Fuller, are reprinted with special permission from St. Martin's Press, Inc., New York. The paraphrase of Mr. J. Krishnamurti's talk given in Saanen, Switzerland, is used by permission of the Krishnamurti Foundation, England. Quotations from *Diet For A New America,* © 1987 by John Robbins, are reprinted with special permission from Stillpoint Publishing, Walpole, NH 03608.

Cover art by Clio Dixon.

ACKNOWLEDGEMENTS

I am grateful for the goodness of the following friends for their assistance in the preparation of this edition of The Future of Mankind:

Lucille Frappier, Charles Johnson, Howard and Bette Schneider, Frank Nader, and Norah Ryan.

I am most grateful to Jim Cheatham for his contribution in editing this book.

CONTENTS

SAFETY

The wish to harm alone engenders fear.
Without it is protection obvious,
And shelter offered everywhere. There is
No time when safety need be sought, no place
Where it is absent, and no circumstance
Which can endanger it in any way.
It is secured by every loving thought,
Made more apparent by each loving glance,
Brought nearer by forgiving words, and kept
Untroubled, cloudless, open to the light,
Redeemed, restored and holy in Christ's sight.*

---

* This poem is from *The Gifts of God* by Dr. Helen Schucman, the Scribe of *A Course In Miracles* (Foundation for Inner Peace, 1982), page 8. It is an incomparable book of poetry containing some of the most important words ever spoken.

INTRODUCTION

LIFE INCONSISTENT with Higher Forces must inevitably result in consequences. The unrealities of commercialized society and the tension and stimulation it produces in an individual's life are detrimental to say the least. These external forces deprive man of the recognition of his real nature.

The purpose of this sharing is to give a background out of which the constructive and positive may emerge. People committed to the status quo change, at best, their point of view. But to see the false as the false demands a change in life and not just a shift in perspective.

We know so little about the intricacies or the laws of fulfillment, of what is internal. Yet rightness and inner conviction will make one independent of the false.

CHAPTER ONE

1

THE CITY
AND LONELINESS

Parents, grandparents, sisters, uncles, aunts, cousins, and nephews all living together in a spacious house – this was my Indian background. The house had one door, which stood as a symbol of unity. For centuries our family had lived in harmony, undivided. Wisdom resided amongst us and lifted us out of irritation and reaction. The elders extended goodness, and children grew up surrounded with affection and a sense of reverence for Life.

No one in the family had ever been career-oriented. We had agricultural land and we were an honored family. We considered ourselves affluent. The family was religious and even without knowing it I absorbed the values of the spirit. Some of us extended ourselves beyond the village – and beyond the boundaries of self-centeredness.

I grew up during India's struggle for independence. Mahatma Gandhi and other leaders of the nation expounded and lived a life of simplicity consistent with the nobleness of non-violence. We learned that the enemy is not always wrong and that you cannot correct wrong with more wrong.

The layman knows little else than the set view of his society. However, one soon gets tired of biases and opinions, the propaganda of prejudice, the fallacy of seeking peace without being at peace.

India gained her independence in 1947 and as a result of the partition and my family's forced migration from Pakistan to India I lost both wealth and property. I came to the United States soon after. The challenge before me was to discover the impact of science on society. The discovery began with the realization: fear is fear; hate is hate, sparing no one; prejudice has no nationality; and everywhere man is the prisoner of memory.

Little did I know of loneliness and all its challenges, or the whirlwind of tension and strong dogmatic belief systems I was to encounter when I came to the New World.

*   *   *

On Christmas Eve of 1947, while still in my twenties, I arrived at La Guardia Airport in New York. I did not know anyone and was a total stranger to the culture of the land. What brought me across the continents was primarily the natural instinct of adventure and exploration. Everything that an exuberant and enterprising phase of life was drawn to experience – wealth, success, sex, fame, knowledge, laughters – attracted me. I was fascinated by newness.

With this introduction to the world of tall sky-scrapers, there also entered into my life, unasked, something I had not known before: loneliness. A profound sense of separation day in and day out, week after week, month after month – a spell of doom. I would walk the streets and ride the subways until I was exhausted. To have no contact or relationship with anyone produces a barren emptiness, worse perhaps than being lost in the Sahara under a blistering sun.

I searched and yearned for human contact but I was too awkward, too alien, too unfamiliar with the ways of the country. In the midst of all the activity it was difficult to get a moment of attention from anyone. I might as well have wished to have a relationship with a bullet in motion or tried to communicate with a bee in a swarm.

A bewildering agony began to gnaw at me day and night. I remember going to a double feature movie every day, on Forty Second Street, sometimes to two showings, just to pass the time. If someone in a department store or restaurant chanced to say a warm "hello" to me, I would walk out of my way to go there just for another "hello." I was so lonely that I would walk miles to see a familiar mulberry tree like the one we had in our garden in India. A tree for a friend. A silent gloom walked with me in my loneliness even though I had money and lived in the Plaza Hotel, one of the most elite settings on Fifth Avenue.

Boredom makes life useless. The search for escape would begin as I woke up and loneliness relentlessly perpetuated it. I would leave my room and stand in front of the hotel, a total stranger, not knowing which way to turn. The pavement and buildings, the shop windows became all too familiar. They seemed to take energy from a person and had nothing to impart but the desire to own objects.

Loneliness accompanied me everywhere. If my feet had eyes they would have left a trail of tears behind. I recall taking a bus from one end of Broadway to the other, and back, hoping to meet someone sitting next to me who would share some words. I would extend a greeting and encourage conversation. Whenever this did happen the response was usually, "Hello, where are you from?" Then the inevitable question about communism, "Is there communism in India?"

The air in a bus is as stale as that of a dogmatic church, or an indoctrinated society. The bus is where I was introduced to nationalism, a disease as depressing as loneliness itself, in which only beliefs and abstract information matter. Strangely enough, people were more interested in what I believed than in who I really was. On political dogma rests your credibility. All of a sudden I was hit with the menace of nationalism. How it loomed into prominence!

For hours at a time, for days in a row, I would stand on a street corner in Times Square hoping to blunder into the familiar face of one of the passengers of the plane on which I had arrived in America. I ate alone, walked alone, slept alone – there was no one with whom to share feelings. Kindness, I was eager to receive and to give, but I was a stranger. There is little human warmth and hospitality where the commercial brain of the city is so preoccupied.

As a result I was annihilated by a menacing force that compelled me to externalize my life. I was not myself anymore. This gloom had power over me. It was a power that violated my existence. I experienced a mild form of hysteria that kept me locked up in the brain and produced an environment of insecurity by which I was affected without knowing it.

I had never before known the hostility of isolation. It seemed a peculiar vibration of this continent. It attacks and then abides in the lives of people but we have become accustomed to it. Its consequences, however, are apt to affect the life of men in all parts of the world. It is so terrifying it produced the atom bomb.

Most of us have known the agony of loneliness and much has been said about the impersonal life in the city, but we never dare to question its roots, especially when we are a feeble stranger under its heel. The stranger is caught in wishes and in his search for relief from loneliness. He does not question – at least, not yet – the purpose of the city that defeats so many people. He is too smothered by its sudden attack. It is like a flu of unknown origin.

The stranger does not question the illusion of the city. To do so he would have to have a voice of his own. We, too, suffer in our malady, overwhelmed by the externals and convinced of our littleness. As long as one remains a bundle of wishes and unfulfillment, one will continue the reign of helplessness upon oneself. How many people are caught in this dilemma!

As you stay in a city you become convinced it is you who have to change, to adjust, to find the means to cope, and even to serve it. The city is dominant in its very nature, a type of monstrosity demanding conformity. Conformed, you are a "citizen."

It is years later one sees – if one ever does – how inconsistent the city is with nature and with the higher values of life. A city the size of New York could have a hundred parks – an avenue of parks and gardens running parallel to the avenues of the traffic; a balance between leisure and activity. To have miles upon miles of concrete covering the earth is a violation. How can the earth breathe?

I began to identify with the cemented earth of the city deprived of sunshine, like death imposed upon life. And here I was in the late 1940's, buried under the loneliness of city life, paying the price for the uncontained lust of curiosity.

I had entered into a world where something in me – the happy whisper – was gone. I was like a corpse that life had discarded. The menace of artificiality was all around me: the streets littered, the houses unloved, the human beings in a state of depression, ever eating. Barren of spirit, pleasure becomes a substitute for happiness, and ideas for gods. There is ever the distance between you and another.

The city, in its artificiality, is impervious to the dawn and twilight. What does it produce that is of life and nature? What does it contribute to the intent and purpose of the soul's relationship with Universal Forces, or with man's highest expression, God, with Whom he is to make his will One? It is a circus of unreality.

At times I would sit quietly in solitary churches where I sensed a peculiar atmosphere, a silence born out of an enclosure untouched by sunlight or the flowing breeze. Here the thoughts and the sorrow of people still lingered.

I would sneak in on Sundays, when the church was full, to hear the minister. I was appalled to discover that he was not a saint but a paid clergyman – a merchant in the pulpit who, after reading from the Bible, wallowed in condemning "godless communism." I was horrified, for the true man of God sees all men created in the image of God. His function is to inspire us out of our prejudices and problems.

The minister was a nationalist, a man subject to circumstances. "THOU SHALT NOT KILL" [1] was evidently not the principle he lived by. He could just as easily bless battleships.

The unproductive middlemen own the city. They buy and sell the unessential. It is a Babylon. [2] And as this middle class that lives off other people grows, so does artificiality. Yet one dare not question the economics of the city. The misconception one has accepted is bigger than the city. The currency states "In God We Trust," [3] but such loneliness prowls the streets. "Where," I asked, "was the Kingdom of God?"

A city is the highly adored pride of nations. The airlines will tell you all about it. It is on display, like a pleasure girl. Endless miles of shops – the city! What is its crop and harvest? Manufactured goods. What, then, would one find in such a superficial atmosphere but loneliness? Loneliness must be its natural outcome.

The lonely have little trust in timeless values. They have been taken out of infinity and put into the separated world of doubt and transition. Doubt is a common habit of mankind. How easily people are affected by it. Not to doubt requires integrity and conviction, a mind of one's own that has mastered its own inconsistencies. We give everything only partial attention. Partial attention lives by doubt. Its very thinking is based on it. Most people read newspapers, listen to TV, or read books just to be informed and keep their biases up to date.

Attachment to our doubts is basic. As long as we can project the "other," we will project our likes and dislikes and our doubts as well. And humanity, groping through a jungle of doubts, is always threatened by something or someone "external." Thus, man never discovers his real thought that is independent of echoes and that trusts in the integrity of Life itself.

Doubt is the inevitable outcome of not being related with the Real. Doubt trusts no one – for long. Where there is a lack of reverence for Life, doubt predominates.

So, here I was in New York, a stranger in a city of doubt. But what lack was there in me that drew me to it? What external influences and propaganda had caught me by this loneliness?

CHAPTER TWO

2

HUMAN CONTACT
BRINGS ABOUT THE "NEW"

IN THE CITY I walked as if in a grave-
yard, with no contact with the living, and I believed it
was "me" who was wrong. So self-convinced are we of
our own inadequacy and littleness against this gigantic conception of a city. Mother Teresa has said that
in America some people are so lonely they want to die.
The city makes one feel like an orphan.

Usually, the first thing people want to know is,
"What do you do for a living?" What is implied in this,
however, is, "Have you acquired a boss yet or not?"
How we suffer to adjust ourselves. Or is it rather that
we have become immune to an atmosphere that lacks
human warmth? You cannot share your feelings with
anyone, for so few have the space and time to listen.

Listen to what Rainer Maria Rilke, the poet, has
written:

"I would like to tell you that Paris was, for me, an experience similar to the military school.

"As great fearful astonishment seized me then, so now again, terror assailed me at everything that, as in an unspeakable confusion, is called life.

"Then I was a boy among boys. I was alone among them, (in the city) and how alone I was, this time among these people. Now perpetually disowned by all I met, the carts drove right through me, and those that were hurrying made no detour about me, but ran over me, full of contempt, as over a bad place in which stagnant water was collecting. It is a big city in which unspeakable things happen. It grew all the time and took the quiet green out of my healing that no longer bears fruit... Houses and streets rose out of the fearful circumstances... And when Paris became, it quickly became very big."

This was my acquaintance with the desperate loneliness of the city, especially in a metropolis like New York.

At this time, museums, concerts, and literature had little meaning for me. I knew very little about the creative spirit of the West. Having attended school for only three years in my entire life, I could barely read. I did speak English, although with an Indian accent. This, too, made things difficult for I had to repeat things over at times, causing me to become self-conscious and painfully shy.

Alone with this loneliness, one day I walked into a bookstore to browse. The owner was a kind man who had studied at Oxford and knew of Tagore, the Indian poet and winner of the Nobel Prize. I was so enchanted by his attention and affection, it lifted me off the ground. How essential and how valuable was this human contact. It brought me to life. It awakened in me a new enthusiasm that led me to buy several hundred dollars worth of books, even though I did not know how to read them. Pocketbooks in those days cost only twenty-five cents, and so you can imagine how many books I bought. Even that did not matter, for the "new" is ever unpredictable, never rational. It is not a child of conformity. It has not yet learned to calculate and is, therefore, spontaneous.

The man in his eagerness started to show me books on India and I said, "I would like to buy those." The response in me was a movement too swift to understand or contain. Another energy awakened in me. Friendship is a dear thing – some heavenly purity when human beings touch each other's hearts. It is like the soothing dewdrops of dawn.

He showed me other books which I had him put aside too. I had heard Greece produced great writers so I asked him, "Do you have anything from Greece?" He said, "Yes." And whatever he showed me I bought. Out of this joyous contact, my thoughts reached out to China, and so I accumulated books on China. And how could I not read of America, the country I was in?

The man in the store was surprised, and so was I, for the books I bought filled many cartons. The question now was: "How are you going to take these with you?" This practical issue had not entered my consciousness. The man brought it up because the time had long passed to close the store. He asked me where I lived. I told him I was staying at the Plaza Hotel and so he delivered the cartons to me there.

When the cartons arrived, I opened them with great excitement and held one book after another in my hands – or was it my own gladness that I was fondling? Little did I know that this was the beginning of a new life for me, a discovery of a new and uncontaminated space that was not of New York, nor of America, nor any place but my own. A relationship was established with the books. I endeavored to make acquaintances with the authors. Slowly I succeeded with some, and not yet with others. But eagerness was alive and an atmosphere of friendship came into being.

My days were lonely, as usual. But I looked forward to the evenings. After dinner, I undressed and sat in bed and relaxed with a book. I discovered the peace and the glory of this relaxation. By relaxation I mean a period that was not intruded upon by projections of wanting to be somewhere other than where I was, nor wanting to be something other than who I was.

When unhappy the mind projects places to visit; it dreams of finding someone on the road. The dissatisfaction within promotes a sense of restlessness. It is totally reliant on the external and on appearances.

As I relaxed it was as if a camel sat down, at peace with nowhere to go. That which I call relaxation not only ended the wishes and the desires, but in some miraculous way, it dissolved the frustration itself and brought me to the peace of the Present.

I sensed that the sole purpose of reading and writing for me, at that time, was to outgrow them and come to something beyond words. I touched upon a much greater Source within me. It was a discovery of an impeccable state in oneself that could directly relate with what it was reading, but not as an idea.

When I read Tolstoy or Socrates, Thoreau or Lao Tzu something else took place because the reading was ever contemplative. It wasn't just reading for information, nor was it reading for memory and the brain. It was reading for the sake of transformation.

One was transformed by this contact with different minds and tremendously grateful. Although the action had begun in India, it was in New York that I began to be awakened from within and touched upon the spirit and sensitivity of Western civilization.

My next important discovery was *how* I actually read. I had not learned to read from another. Although unlettered with only three years of education, I taught myself to read and write. And now the non-pressured atmosphere of awakened interest evolved its own way of reading which was fundamentally different from that of schools.

The reading one learns in schools merely serves to train the brain to function like a computer, and the faster the better. But this other reading was very different. I could not read more than two or three pages an hour. And when I was *able* to read faster, the reading became even slower. I would be hit by the impact of what was written and it would often take me forty-five minutes just with one paragraph. I could not read what Lao Tzu had to say and pass it by; I wanted to make contact with its truth. And that is what transformed.

I find there are exceptionally few people who know how to read, for their reading is limited to their own thought system and not to the silence beyond the words where separation ends.

What makes this reading different is the space that accompanies it. At one level it is not a reading at all but a communication with the very creative spirit of the author who may have lived a century ago. It is the approach of the timeless mind to reading. This quality of reading is the one that outgrows what it reads. It has a direct relationship with that which is not of time and often surpasses the author himself in its perfection. Thus, writing, even at its most sublime, seems an indulgence.

The period that followed was a flowering of being with the essential. It was my naive conviction, then, that what you read was to be lived. Imagine what Thoreau's *Walden* would do! His essay on walking transformed my life; I walked everywhere. Without application reading is hypocrisy. It is an activity devoid of action.

Now I felt at home, boundless and as creative as the Present. Out of the desperation of my life a flower had bloomed and for three years I basked in the serene glory of aloneness. Each night from 8:00 PM until 2:00 or 3:00 AM, I would read. There was no pressure or haste, and it allowed me to,

> "Leap into the breath
> that takes no heed of you."
> WALT WHITMAN

I began to question the authority of my own thought and the belief in other men's ideas. Something was awakening, a new intelligence – with its own determination not to compromise. There grew the need for a state of being that is holy and truly religious, a life of virtue, free of illusions, ever in harmony with the universe.

This was the beginning of a resolve never to work for another, nor ever to take advantage. At times I was in dire crisis, but out of this emerged moments of freedom from memory, sublime touches of peace, an alive intensity of the moment when time ceases and everything in creation is blessed. This transformed my loneliness to the joy of aloneness. In these eternal moments it was bliss to be ALONE, and nothing was external to oneself.

* * *

Learning to read was a transformation, not just an activity. It made my life productive. The loneliness I had experienced was from not knowing what to do. There was curiosity seeking pleasurable activity, and gratification wanting to be pacified. But even that preoccupation would invariably become a routine and the need for outlets would continue just the same.

The action of reading was the awakening of interest. Interest has its own intrinsic value, a completeness of its own that imparts happiness – the real nature of life – which supersedes the stimulation of the senses. We try to escape loneliness but as George Bernard Shaw would say, "We remain intentionally dull," with the spirit still dormant.

In India loneliness was not so haunting, for there is the extended family system. People in general have fewer barriers and are more humanistic. Perhaps it is this humanism that made it possible for India to survive over the centuries in spite of all its ups and downs. With a culture that abounded in hospitality it had no need of hotels and restaurants.

Coming from such a background to its total opposite – the lonely, impersonal life of the city – was quite a shock. And yet at the time I dared not be honest with myself. I was so overwhelmed by what I had been convinced of: the city is beyond reproach. The little "me" must never question it. How "bigness" thwarts the individual!

Who can be honest without being successful according to the city's terms? Yet honesty is in-dependent. How can you be honest if you are not free? Is success determined by owning things or is it by being with the purpose of your life? Can you be successful with the externals, always wanting more? There are men who cannot be owned by anything.

They are bigger than the city and the country. Their lives are the real civilizing factors in society.

The welcoming voices of Whitman, Emerson, Thoreau, and Lincoln came, like grace, to introduce one to eternity.

"I am larger, better than I thought. I did not know I held so much goodness... I depart from materiality. I am as one disembodied."

WALT WHITMAN

"Whosoever would be a man, must be a nonconformist. He who would gather mortal palms must not be hindered by the name of goodness. Nothing is at last sacred but the integrity of your own mind. Absolve you to yourself, and you shall have the suffrage of the world."

RALPH WALDO EMERSON

"Cultivate poverty like sage, like a garden herb. Do not trouble yourself to get new things, whether clothes or friends. That is dissipation. Turn the old, return to them. Things do not change; we change. If I were confined to a corner in a garret all my days, like a spider, the world would be just as large to me while I had my thoughts."

HENRY DAVID THOREAU

These are the voices of some of those who have broken through the mirage of the external and have come to their own non-sensational "newness."

The solitary hours of reading provided the space for this awakening. "Solitude is the school of genius," a poet has said. The mystic adores it.

In what way does the external system of education help or contribute to the awakening of newness and purity in a man or in a child? Conventional schooling serves its system of separation from God, man, and nature, rather than integration with Universal Forces. What price we pay for this ignorance! Yet all the planetary forces are focused in man. He is universal. Such is his infinity.

Man is beguiled out of his true identity and his divinity in order to serve the manmade systems of commerce and politics and the fallacy of nationalism. The price of this education of the external is that we have lost our innocence. Is this not too high a price to pay?

The price is the deep-seated unfulfillment pre-valent amongst most people. It seems as if everyone is seeking his own appeasement in the externals. The externals have become more important than the human being in our culture of "me" and "mine." But we will not remain satisfied with these for long. From disillusion to disillusion we gather experience to be cynical and frustrated in our old age.

> "The world of senses is the world of shows.
> It does not exist for itself."
> RALPH WALDO EMERSON

In the spacious aloneness of night, giving birth to dawn, I questioned the authenticity of organized, professional religions that blessed the battleships, cast out saints, persecuted the holy, and yet did nothing about the deep-seated fear and anxiety in man. I questioned the wisdom of a society where most people were someone else's employees.

"Can man live by bread alone?"
FEODOR DOSTOEVSKI

Thus began my self-education. These hours of inspiration were a gift of God. I began to outgrow the sugar-coated words of the sentimental poets and authors, and walked with the glad goodness of Whitman and the simple purity of Thoreau. I got to know America by knowing Jefferson and Emerson; and China by knowing Lao Tzu and Chuang Tzu.

"We never buy more than we need.
We never need more than we use.
We never use more than it takes to get by,
Until we learn to need less."
CHINESE PROVERB

During these solitary hours of spacious aloneness I would expand and travel to Persia, the land of Hafiz and Rumi; to the sensitivity of the Pharaohs and the holiness of Hebrew prophets. And there were the giants of Russia – Tolstoy and Dostoevski; of France – Andre Gide, Cocteau, and Sartre. There was the Italian Renaissance, and the music of Bach, Beethoven, and Sibelius. There was George Bernard Shaw and Joan of Arc; Bertrand Russell and Sir Thomas More; Henry Miller and Florence Nightingale; D.H. Lawrence and Dylan Thomas – all these and their voices now walked with me. Concerts opened their doors; museums, their splendor; and theatre, its living creativity.

I also discovered the treasures of my own native country: Sri Ramana Maharshi, Sri Ramakrishna, Kalidas, Ananda Coomaraswamy, the *Ramayana*, the *Bhagavad Gita*, and the *Dhammapada* of Lord Buddha, the writings of Jawaharlal Nehru, as well as the sacred presence of Guru Nanak trodding across countries with his celestial message.

My fate must have changed, for my taste in clothes and food and places changed. I now had something of my own to say. Occasionally, I would hear "my own voice" that was no longer an echo of others. And with that came the discrimination to recognize the men of clear voices and the masses caught in choices.

In silence one evolved and grew into dimensions beyond the reaches of activity. This opened yet other doors. Where there is discrimination there is the recognition of who you are. Having my own voice led me to acquaintances with those who were the voices of the age. I met with Mrs. Eleanor Roosevelt, with whom I stayed in Hyde Park. I also met with Helen Keller, Aldous and Maria Huxley, the wise and unpretentious Mark Van Doren, and Chief Justice William O. Douglas. People would ask me how I was able to meet "so and so"? How could I explain that I met them in moments of silence where I grew a century and, therefore, had something to say that related me to them? It was meeting the sensitivity within me that introduced me to those of universal outlook.

The city generates an enormous energy and draws to itself people from all over the world. It has much to impart: professionalism and sophistication, cultural events, museums, and concerts; and in it one finds men and women of excellence. It is usually out of the city that an anthropologist evolves who explores the dark recesses of Africa or the wastelands of Australia. Out of the city emerge writers, poets, painters, and musicians.

It is in New York City that I first met the God-lit Mr. J. Krishnamurti. [1] The holy prophet Nanak had said,

> "If a hundred moons were to rise and a thousand suns multiplied, even that intensity of light will not dispel ignorance." [2]

It is the God-lit man who illumines the darkness. The meeting with Mr. Krishnamurti, in a matter of minutes, awakened within me that which is eternal. A decade later, again in the city of New York, I met with the shining light of *A Course In Miracles*, Dr. Helen Schucman. [3]

A Course In Miracles dispels the illusion of words and ideas by which we are brainwashed. It relates one to the truth, the fact, the direct experience of what is real. This contact with *A Course In Miracles* introduced me to the fulfillment of my destiny.

And so we see that the city does have keys to impart. It is a place where one comes to be charged and to receive. If this has taken place, then this energy takes one out of the city, and wherever you go you too will have something to impart.

The city puts its foot on your face and makes you conform if you do not outgrow it. In time it can become stagnant and the people in it as non-energetic as the slums. It is tragic if a person continues to stay in the city, for one does not build a home on a bridge.

CHAPTER THREE

3

FROM THE CITY
TO THE VEDIC AGE
OF SHINING BEINGS
EXTENDING THE WILL OF GOD

WE HAVE TALKED about the loneliness of the city and have observed what it does and reveals. Let us see if the rural area – the alternative to urban society – has been better able to cope with the forces that are swaying humanity.

> "The village communities are little republics, having nearly everything they want within themselves, and almost independent of foreign relations. They seem to last where nothing else lasts. This union of the village communities, each one forming a separate little state by itself...is in a high degree conducive to their happiness and to the enjoyment of a great portion of freedom and independence."
>
> SIR GEORGE MERCOLFE,
> British Governor of India

The villages of India alone amount to over five hundred thousand and, until recent generations, had no police stations. They were self-sufficient.

The pace in the life of the village is obviously less hectic than in the city, but only in the sense that distractions are not yet accessible to it. Its naivete and innocence are like that of a child.

As he grows a child is attracted by and goes after new and colorful things. We can observe this same process as village meets city. To the non-sophisticated villager a city symbolizes a kind of satisfaction, a sense of improvement, and the joy of gratification. The city has an enticing aura of distraction. It sets the restlessness of seeking aflame.

In the beginning the city offered cathedrals and temples, a greater variety of goods, culture, art, and expression. It served certain kinds of academic and cultural aspirations such as dance, painting, and singing.

This standard, however, is not maintained as the city spreads. More energetic, more impersonal, it produces things for the gratification of man. City dwellers have more things but, at the same time, their needs increase. Wishing and wanting become more dominant in their lives and outlets more accessible. The extension of unfulfillment is the history of man. People like Napoleon and Alexander and Genghis Khan become the "great men" of history, the heroes.

Today we see monopolies taking over the free enterprise economy and society. Overnight the

7-Eleven stores spread all over the country. Radio Shack, Wal-Mart, McDonald's, Taco Bell, other chain restaurants and department stores multiply. Extending itself like a creeper, monopoly goes into the rural areas.

The rural areas, at first, are passive and dormant. But latent unfulfillment begins to awaken and the non-sophisticated rural life is then challenged and destroyed. Where the pace had been slow, the spread of unfulfillment ends up being the most rapid. Overnight people are mesmerized by the fast pace of the media and sales techniques. Social trends change local customs. Traditions are weakened.

This shift reveals that the agrarian dwellers may not have been as happy as they pretended to be. Banks, lawyers, doctors migrate into the village areas and pretty soon the world that was mostly villages with a few cities now becomes more cities and fewer villages. Slowly the village is being invaded out of existence.

There is essentially no difference between the village and the city, for the destructive tendencies of unfulfillment exist in both. No matter how impressive or expensive they may appear, changes in education, etiquette, prosperity, language, and dress are still external and do not originate from inner peace. Where have they led man?

Where relationship was based on simple survival, the family stuck together. Farmers were farmers, potters were potters, carpenters remained carpenters, and they passed on their craft. But in the momentum of today's "progress," man is isolated from man. The world has become a place of consumers and money its most important factor – like the circulation of blood in the body.

Even in the underdeveloped countries of the world, "job" has become the issue of survival in life. Better wages become a necessity. All over the world the manufacture of armament provides jobs. To kill becomes a necessity.

The trend from self-employment to working for hire is apt to prove most destructive in the long run. In it lies the loss of man's own identity. Man's external knowledge makes a living, holds the jobs, and maintains the routine, but in it there is less and less need of wisdom. Faith and trust have lost their validity as skills and abilities have taken their place. The media form the opinions of the people and tell them what to buy, what to do, and how to think. And so the destructiveness of unfulfillment continues.

In today's world, women seeking equality have become equal – but now they have to work. Femininity is all but lost and mothers have become career women. Divorce is rampant. More and more children grow up without a father. Women have achieved equality; and men, quite content with their own nomadic nature, have gained freedom. The break-up of families has made women more vulnerable than ever. First they were suppressed; now they are abused.

This is the age of computers and electronics. Though man's brain is trained to develop certain faculties and function like a machine, it cannot compete with the computer which is far superior. These professional brains can outwit the brains of ordinary individuals and, as a result, the latter conform to those of vested interest. Thus the human being becomes less and less important, the system all-important.

When artificiality prevails, no city is much different from any other city. Variety gives way to sameness. Airports, hotels, waiters, taxis, radios, advertisements seem very much alike. Society becomes highly conditioned.

For the most part, you are only what the city allows you to be. Think about this and the truth begins to unfold in you. Then it is your own discovery, no longer someone else's idea.

You are allowed to be what your training credentials say you are. Status and advantage are the city's sanctions and may have no validity other than in society. By being merely what the city allows you to be you are deprived of the vastness of your own reality. Most of society is forever prevented from knowing what is eternal – love, truth, relationship. What a bleak existence!

We live in the ignorance of the "known" and rarely discover the newness of the Present. We live in a world of efficiency and greed and fear. Insecurity allows us no space to live in the Kingdom of God. The ideas with which we are brainwashed mask who we are. Our own knowing has become detrimental.

First the outsider, the conqueror, used to exploit the conquered and had colonies. Today we are exploited by our own society. There is not much anyone can do about taxes and the expenses of war. The individual ends up paying, usually without knowing he is being billed. And the price we pay is very high.

Humanity is tired and most individuals' lives are in disorder. There is such restlessness and busyness that we are exhausted as never before, for we live by an unnatural, commercial rhythm. It is only the illusion of living and not the extension of Life, the holiness of eternity. Yet ...*there is a point beyond which illusions cannot go.* [1]

Everything at the level of personality is unreal because it is part of the externals. Times will reveal that we cannot depend on the externals. The twelfth hour is upon man. Neither armament, nor commercialization, nor politics will bring a transformation. Humanity shifts from one to the other, with no difference whatsoever, for at the bottom of each is personal insecurity.

Fear rules where there is lack of awareness. Awareness is the uneducated light within. As this vitality diminishes we become prey to propaganda and commercial manipulation. Where is reverence for the human being who bears the universe within himself?

*   *   *

It is still possible for the individual to take responsibility and step out of the deceptions and illusions in which society is caught. Each one of us can step out of the mania of self-improvement and the fragmentation of nationalism, religious dogma, and economic theory – all founded on insecurity.

Limitations are not real. We could outgrow them in an instant if we did not believe in postponement. Knowledge of Reality is absolute and it is accessible every instant.

For guidance, let us look into the lifestyle of the Vedic sages, or rishis, of the Golden Age, of the sages of the Upanishads,* and of the Essenes.+

In the Vedic Age – before the advent of the all-wise Noah [2] – beings lived upon the earth who were not confined to the body senses. These hermits – or forest dwellers, as they were sometimes called – were highly evolved. Their integrity was equal to that of celestial beings and archangels. They witnessed the world of glory and sang the praise and joy of heaven from which they never departed. They never separated from totality into time.

---

* Because time is seen as a concept, as illusion or unreality, the Golden Age is a term not limited to chronological time. A sage or rishi – general terms for saints or seers – is one who abides in the ever-present eternity of the NOW which does not change. Therefore,the Vedas represent a timeless age of God-perspective, and are the most ancient scriptures of the Hindus, regarded by the orthodox as direct revelation and supreme authority in all religious matters. The Upanishads are the sacred scriptures which constitute the philosophical portion of the Vedas and, by teaching the knowledge of God, record the spiritual experiences of the sages of ancient India.

+ The Essenes were an ancient Jewish sect that existed between the second century B.C. and the second century A.D. which stressed rigorous asceticism and a distinctive form of mysticism. For further information on the Essenes, see *The Qumran Community* by Charles T. Fritsch (MacMillan Company, 1956).

These sages had but one ethic, the one truth that man is the altar of God in the world and brings the Kingdom of God to earth. This enables the Grace of God to surround creation. Their purity of being enriched the very Prana* of creation.

These mystics were beyond the limitations of thought. Their actions were born out of fulfillment. They had nothing to achieve. Because their lives were not confined to the body, each remained an altar of Heaven reaching beyond the universe. They lived consistent with the Will of God and chose never to deviate into alternatives. Thus, they were ever with the justice of love and forgiveness. The limitations of space and distance were not upon them, for their state of being was beyond cause and effect. Having no attachments they bore no burden of the flesh. They sensed no lack in themselves or in creation, and were enraptured by the perfection and glory of every tree and leaf, star and animal.

Because the sages of the Vedic Age were not earth-bound they had no need to develop agriculture. In fact, they themselves were masters of the natural world. Creation existed for them, and they commanded it what to do. Their needs were met by the blessing they conferred upon nature.

Nature, as the expression of earth energies, is in itself competitive, aggressive, and often destructive. It maintains its vitality through friction. It is man who

---

* Prana: The sum total of primal energy, from which all mental and physical energy has evolved. Prana is the vital principle which sustains physical life, thought force, and bodily action. – *Vedanta And The West* by Brahmacharini Usha (Vedanta Press, 1962), page 55.

brings the peace of non-duality to all that is earth-born.

Animals are part of the earth energies; and man is, too, as long as he is limited to the body. Nourished and provided for by the earth forces, he remains ferocious unless he rises to his natural Self, which is the pre-body state.

When man lost this clear vision a sense of lack descended upon him and self-survival added its first weight. Out of his insecurity came the advent of agriculture – and the beginning of his decline. Limitedness grew stronger over a gradual process of centuries. Identification with the body and its sensations, choices, and preferences continued to widen the gap between his natural Self and the ego self all through the ages. And now, man is almost totally bound to his physicality and is dedicated to ownership.

Since the fall of man into limited existence, he has nearly lost the memory of God. Space and time are now the assumed realities in which we live and breathe. Yet, in reality, there is no space or time, no lack, or even loss of memory of God and Oneness. That which is real is never affected, nor can it be changed. It still is as it has been eternally.

The forest dwellers and sages were men of virtuous refinement and sensitivity. By discovering how Eternal Laws were abused, they found the key to correcting their alignment. The means of restoring the perfection in man was to discover the abuse instantly. Therefore, helplessness never touched them and their lives remained a blessing upon the planet. Nor did they acknowledge death or give it authority.

Kings sat at their feet to receive counsel. From them they learned to maintain truth and give integrity to their words. Kings and queens and princes, as well as the wise minds of the world, visited the hermitages and often came to stay there in the later phase of their lives, leaving the throne to dedicate themselves to divine Will. There are accounts of these encounters and episodes in the ancient scriptures and sacred writings.

The holy abodes of the sages speak of the innocent purity of their lives. In his masterpiece, the Sanskrit play, *Shakuntala*, Kalidas tells us of a king on his hunt, in his swift and dazzling chariot, chasing an antelope through the forest. And there came the vertical voice of a sage, powerful like lightning:

> "Stop! These are sacred grounds. The antelope is not a paper toy for you to set fire to. Restore your weapon to its quiver. Your arms are to shield the weak rather than to bring anguish on the innocent."

The vertical voice of the sage, who is consistent at all levels of his being, is a Law unto itself. It is a voice at once external for the physical ears to hear, and internal, for it is of Life.

The king heeded. "I am sorry," he pleaded as he got off his chariot and stood in wonder. The dazzling, speeding chariot represents the acceleration of future ages and how its arrogance and ignorance will invade the God-given serenity, peace, and fulfillment of man.

After the Vedic Age came the period of the Upanishads. The holy beings of this time lived on sacred sites near rivers and lakes. All-knowing were they about ley lines, power points, currents of the earth, and vibrations. They were men of direct knowing and masters of music, astronomy, mathematics, and medicine – the laws that constitute the manifest world.

Free of spirit, knowers of Pranic energies, and living chaste lives, what the sages manifested on the physical plane was what first took place at higher planes. The work was completed before the activity was done. These beings, too, were not bound to agriculture. Theirs was the power of invocation – the power of Heaven.

> "The Vedas and all their accessory literatures and sciences, for example, are contained in the word which, having been uttered is then heard by the prophets, that audition depending not on 'inspiration' but upon 'attention.'"
>
> ANANDA K. COOMARASWAMY

The holy rishis were one with the Mind of God and could perceive the processions of eons in an instant. Their lives were consistent extensions of the Word of God.

Following the Vedic Age and the period of the Upanishads we come to the Essenes – men and women of detachment who lived mostly by the natural laws of economy, creation, and the seasons. The action of the Essenes is a timeless statement that proves each individual can realize truth and extend the reality of God to others. Let us not look at their story "historically," but rather with the intent to inherit the vitality of the life of virtue these shining beings extended. The Essenes existed prior to the advent of Jesus. Their ethics were opposed to artificial divisions and the corrupting influence of worldliness which undermined the honesty of the human being. They were incorruptible men and women who spoke the truth.

The Essenes, too, lived by Divine Laws. They lived without the authority of a leader, a figurehead, and without personal ownership. They were devotional men and women who dedicated their lives to transcending work itself. Amongst them, no work was considered superior to another person's. Each person was given equal opportunity and each practiced it according to his conscience.

They did not live off the energy of another person's money. They never commercialized their lives, nor did they resort to barter, personal gain, or advantage. They would not buy the goods of one man and sell them to another; each created and shared what he produced. Some of the Essenes, known as the Theraputae, practiced medicine and healed the sick free of charge. What an opportunity to learn of the resources of giving. Right action is complete unto itself and a good deed is its own compensation.

The Essenes excelled in thoughtfulness and gratitude, and came to symbolize peace, goodness, and tenderness. They rested in silence and brought prayers into application. Remarkably, they outgrew their own order and dissolved it when their work was done. Once orthodoxy began to set in, they disbanded and became anonymous.

The Essenes did not do one thing for the sake of something else. Their intrinsic life was without conflict. Their dedication to truth made their lives impersonal, permitting the light within to flow forth into more perfect expression, thereby making the body the means of the spirit.

Is this not the challenge for each of us: to discover our own identity? This done, our function becomes consistent and, therefore, effortless.

The issue today is that each of us is confronted with the conformity of self-survival. Can we cope with the pressures and stimulation of the externals?

Mysticism is an experience of inner strength within oneself, making virtue possible and the "Given" accessible. But progress, instead, has introduced distraction into our consciousness as a block against self-knowing, thus overshadowing our co-creator-ship. External systems have done nothing about our reactions, fear, or insecurity. They have merely facilitated the means to implement them.

Non-commercialized life alone will succeed and be able to cope with what is ahead for the externalized world. The city would not survive if there were not a few people whose vertical lives extend the Grace of God on earth.

It is apparent that the system cannot change. However, the individual can. He can undo his conditioning simply by not giving it authority and by questioning his own conclusions. He must question the authority he has imposed upon himself with his own unrealized words. The vitality is in the question. The very questioning will awaken him to the potentials within. Truth is never helpless. Seeing the false as the false will liberate him.

Change of situations will not help, for at the relative level there is no perfect situation. The earnest person, seeing the problem itself, comes to an urgency and seriousness that dissolve the fallacy of ideas and ideals.

This process of inner awakening is independent of the externals and therefore, not impeded by them. The question is the passion of your own genuine interest. Self-reliance has its own potential; it never underestimates itself.

One comes to flowering by the discovery of one's own holiness. Everything in creation exists to bring man to perfection.

CHAPTER FOUR

4

THE HUMAN CRISIS –
THE GAP IS INCREASING

THE CITY IN ITSELF is an enlarged ego. Is this ego enlarged as a mechanism of self-preservation and self-interest?

There is only one Source of life. Everything that lives extends and expands. For example, the tree produces a whole crop of seeds and is consistent with this law. The love and truth that sustain life are our perfection to extend.

In the separated state we cannot create, but we can project and give value to what we make. Therefore, we suffer from our own misperceptions. The city is a child of our inner separation. Through the isolation of fear and anxiety, the city extends and expands our separation from nature. Knowing this we must realize the implications of what we have initiated.

The slums of New York City will not only continue they will get worse, regardless of riches the city might amass. Drugs and violence will proliferate no matter how much the city or the Federal Government try to contain them. The gap between the rich and the poor is widening and there will be slums of staggering proportions. Since growth and expansion will not stop, war is inevitable. It is the industrial economy's most profitable solution and quite acceptable to the collective consciousness.

Industrialists, political leaders, heads of organized religions, and militarists think alike, for the secondary man is in the forefront, having in his power the ability to drain human energy into a "King Kong" of affluence. It is an artificial affluence. Without peace within we are caught in a world of appearances – the slavery of separation from our Source. A collective consciousness that is limited to physical sensation can be exploited. The system can improve and even perfect technology, but slums are its creation as well. Affluence and decadence go hand in hand.

BUT TO THE SEER ALONE,
THE EFFECTS UNFOLD THE INVISIBLE CAUSE.

The city is by nature seductive, and in the long run self-destructive, for it is unnatural. We see this in the large number of people who congregate in one area. A concentrated city of ten million people, with no farm land surrounding it, is dependent on transportation for food from faraway places, the transportation often costing more than the product itself. It is not the city that sustains the human being but the countryside with its ever-productive earth. And some day the waste of human energy will catch up.

Skyscrapers, owned by rich corporations, are built with human energy. Yet the human being does not have a place of his own. The trend now is to own a car and to work for another rather than to own a home. Without a home children grow up without roots. What could be more important than the individual and sociological atmosphere of a home, where children can grow up with gardens and flower beds of their own? It would be a place for reunion, a place to be in the sunlight with the songs of birds and friends. A law providing every citizen with a home – so that there are no tenants – would bring about a system of newness, consistent with the New World consciousness.

Outrageous, you may say, all the while approving of the corporate skyscrapers and profiteers with incomes as great as some of the nations of the world. The wealth they have amassed is phenomenal; they virtually own the sky, the oceans, and the earth, along with the human beings who live upon it. Certainly we can afford to give children a place to establish their roots so their parents are not haunted by the monthly rent that compels them to be wage-earners. Insecurity produces careers that prevent the intrinsic expression of one's Beingness. Most of the population today produces unessential things.

The city is built by exploitative minds. They subject themselves – and all of us – to the dictates of "thought, then action," with a wide gap in between sustained by the energy of conflict.

The city is where the personality ordeal is all-consuming. Simplicity is annihilated by dependence. Stimulation dominates our lives and influences our choices of food, profession, and relationships. It subjects us to habit and sensation. In the absence of relaxation and serenity, our activities are dominated by the quest for survival and gratification; our pursuit of pleasure is in direct relationship to our increasing sense of insecurity and fear. An artificial life of conflict attempts to escape from fear through pleasure.

"Bigness" is sustained by accelerated growth. The consequences of this acceleration are alarming. It is self-destructive. The industrial empire spreads by first arousing appetites and then by appeasing those appetites with manufactured products. Thus, one always needs money. And so the gap between nations, between the "haves" and the "have-nots," builds.

There is another ever-widening gap that is even more sinister: the gap between the average person and those who have control over him. The electronic technology of vested interests is so swift and imperceptible in its subliminal effects that the layman is taken in without knowing it. The commercial world has its illusionary territorial rights over the populace.

This is more serious than we realize. It is not only an abuse of nature or an exploitation of markets, it is a manipulation of the human being himself. Henry James said, "I am often struck at the limitation with which men of power pay the price for their domination over mankind."

More and more we are being limited to the "known," to the appetites and the bondage of physicality. Our function is limited to mere routine. We are enslaved by the industrial economy. As this invasion upon our freedom continues, something natural – the spontaneous within us – is being destroyed.

Violation on such a massive scale brings an unforeseen contamination of human consciousness which affects the very atmosphere that surrounds the earth. The crust of the earth and human consciousness are related. The thin layer that surrounds the globe where life exists is an extension of human consciousness and is affected by it.

Even our ability to question is becoming limited. Our choices fall within the realm of duality. In this most affluent society most people are woefully low on money and thus confined to their milieu. Education, for the most part, prepares us to fit in and serve the system. How many of us are confined to being wage earners? Banks, telephone companies, insurance corporations, have the last word.

In the city, where nearly everyone is an employee, few can afford a home. But the nation can afford war and aggression! The city can afford tobacco companies but not "LOVE YE ONE ANOTHER." [1] Tobacco companies can afford to provide hundreds of parks, avenues of flower beds, and trees. Instead, cigarettes are the main crop of the city. What, then, is our affluence? Is it not what Henry David Thoreau called,

"...improved means to an unimproved end"?

Heed the farsighted words of Abraham Lincoln:

"Prosperity breeds tyrants."

Our perception is either true or false. But do we not see how discernment, the most valuable gift of heaven, is taken away from us and we do not even know it?

God did not create a meaningless world. [2]

For generations man has been made helpless by his lack of awareness of the purity of all-knowing Innocence. Innocence is too wise to get tangled up in the ways of man. It knows God as the Creator, the Father, the creative Force behind manifestation, the Sustainer of life, the Light beyond perception.

I want to point out that I am not speaking of socialism, communism, or capitalism. These are man-made. My primary interest is in man's relationship with his eternal Self, not his economic or political views. Of course, external conditions are important and cannot be underestimated; but the Source of physical senses is divine to me.

Having come from India to America I was all too aware that it is a fallacy to seek political peace without having internal peace. The discovery of the impact of science on society was vital to me.

Man's instinctive nature is good. Of this I had no doubt. Since I saw all men as good I could not accept the "enemy" as bad. My concern was with the factors that mislead man, for once confused, his clarity is lost. I saw that man's life was too externalized and that the media generated influence and increased misinformation. The daily newspapers fostered a hysteria, fear, and frustration, and contributed to the imbalances in man. The media and its propaganda were very commercial.

I questioned prosperity. Did it increase or decrease the distance between man and his divine nature? Did science and prosperity contribute to virtue, ethics, or the dignity of man? I wondered if better relationships between the nations of the East and the West would help. In fact, this later became a passion with me and brought me in contact with men and women whose lives were intrinsic and who valued the goodness of man. Peace and goodness are not found outside oneself and then brought in; what is within us reaches out and beyond.

I view man as a co-creator with God. The planet welcomes his presence, which brings to it the vibration of the Kingdom of Heaven. Manmade rules and values are "horizontal." I am looking at the "vertical" man who is pressured to conform in this so-called land of new consciousness.

Although I have been to almost all of the great cities of the world, I am not comparing. Direct comprehension does not compare. Mine is a question. In what way is the New World new? According to Divine Law, everything extends itself. Where is the thinking that originates from the creativity of love and peace, or from the Mind of God? In what way has the New World awakened to, "THY WILL BE DONE ON EARTH AS IT IS IN HEAVEN"? [3]

Here in the New World, as elsewhere, we are caught in the self-centeredness of the images of thought preoccupied with survival. Even our educational institutions and organized religions are sustained by the energy of friction, based as they are on limited, physical senses. They do not awaken us to wholeness. Yet love is the law.

Our inner purity changes all circumstances; we are not helpless. Nothing external can control us. As long as we try to exploit another, however, we violate the Eternal Law and are subject to consequences. How expensive the consequences have become!

> "Let us have faith that right makes might, and in that faith, let us, to the end, dare to do our duty...
>
> "Let us strive to deserve...the continued care of Divine Providence, trusting that, in future national emergencies, He will not fail to provide us the instruments of safety and security.
>
> "Destroy that spirit, and you have planted the seeds of despotism around your own doors."   ABRAHAM LINCOLN

These words, then, are not political. They are the statement of a vertical man who is not swayed by circumstances.

*   *   *

Agrarian societies produced saints in ancient times and urban civilization has produced geniuses of the creative arts. But the vast majority of the population has remained subject to conformity.

"Yesterday" and "tomorrow" are projections of the human brain and are not a reality at all. Whether we are in the city or in the village we live by the same misconceptions. We can see the similarity behind their obvious differences.

We have dwelt enough on the city and on the pastoral lifestyle of the rural communities. Now, outgrowing both village and city is our primary concern. The important thing is man's discovery of himself and his identity with God. This makes the external issues secondary. Whether rural or urban, the life of external preferences is common to both. The fact is, however, where there is choice, there is no freedom. Self-centeredness is the origin of contradiction and conflict upon the planet.

We need to establish the very foundation and purpose of man on earth. And we need to take the stand that will end the separation between man and man and between man and God; and come to the union, the wholeness of the One Life we all share.

PRESENT IS PRESENT.

GOD IS.

YOU ARE NOT SEPARATED, BUT INDEPENDENT,
AS LOVE IS INDEPENDENT.

Cities and villages of the world are caught in the misconceptions of solving the self-created problems of insecurity and separation. What has man's culture done to bring the individual to the peace of God or the reality of the Light that he is? What is so lofty about any culture that drafts its citizens to wage war and uses its economy as a means of self-destruction?

Fortunately, ignorance is not eternal. Man, today, as harassed as he is by unfulfillment and its consequences, can surely outgrow the illusion of external nothingness. Time has no effect on his eternity. Nor is he any less holy than as God created him. Love cannot be afraid. Its radiance rekindles and increases in joy. Natural intelligence is effortless. It is not timebound.

The personality of man is conditioned, but it has no power over the eternity of man. Unless you surrender to it. The choice is yours.

Knowing you are sustained by the Love of God, you, too, out of the gratefulness of your heart, can join the chorus of everything in creation singing the glory of its own perfection in praise of the Creator.

CHAPTER FIVE

5

AMERICA'S DESTINY

AN INDIAN VILLAGER does not visit psychologists or lawyers when he has a problem. He goes to a saint or holy person, a relative or a neighbor who is at peace. Such persons have values beyond "me and mine," and when talking with them something is shared which is not limited to the personal. Although there is not much money in that part of the world, there is humanism.

In the evening you could go for a walk together in the fields. Lovingly your friend would then invite you to talk saying, "Come. Sit down." Whatever your concerns, they would be dissolved. Being "backward," sometimes the villagers are unaware even of who the Prime Minister is, but they can be very wise. "God is our ruler," they would state, "these others come and go."

Instead of producing politicians, such a country brings forth leaders who are giants of ethics and

71

values. There were several of these wise men of intrinsic life and consistent knowledge who made a strong impact on my life. One of the most extraordinary was Giani Kartar Singh. I met him on a train at Amritsar on the way to Lahore in 1945.

He came and sat opposite me in the compartment. I was in crisis, burning to make contact and not knowing how to approach him. But the energy of first thought acts involuntarily. Gianiji, an eminent man, was the leader of the Sikhs. His Sikhism encompassed all humanity in its range; his nationalism was unlimited humanism.

Gianiji was a man of renunciation and religious outlook who never had a bank account. His life was completely simple and given to service. It is he who taught me humanism. The force of his love transformed my life, and in his atmosphere I blossomed. He offered an intimate relationship through which I became a friend of Prime Minister Nehru and others of incorruptible lives. When people asked him, "What do you see in Tara Singh?" Gianiji would say:

> "The word 'impossible' does not apply to him. He will not accept second best and this will make him or break him."

This contact with the wise opened totally new dimensions and potentials within me and made things possible in an India besieged by the cruelty of poverty. It culminated in an enormous industrial project at the grassroots level with capital of over six million dollars supported by Sikhs, maharajahs, and others – but most of all by Gianiji's impeccable integrity.

In 1947, however, the advent of freedom and the partition of India and Pakistan disrupted this humanistic plan. Before embarking upon another venture I felt the need to visit the West to make an individual survey of the impact of science on society. One questioned what part the world's underdeveloped, agrarian society of almost two billion was to play in the Post-War period.

When the British granted India its freedom the wise were asked to formulate its Constitution, and an untouchable was made the head of the committee. Gianiji led the constitutional committee on minorities and democracy; I was one of his assistants. We studied the examples of Switzerland and French Quebec to find ways of dealing with these issues.

Before coming to America one had discovered how the British exploited the colonies. But so did the native Indian kings, or maharajahs. Five million Indians died of starvation in the early 1900's. "Wages are going down instead of up," wrote Swami Rama Tirtha, "notwithstanding the increase of industries, the extension of railway systems, and other sources of wealth and employment that are being rapidly developed." [1]

Britain demanded more from India than the country could give, and so the colony's debt rose from 51 million pounds in 1857 to 200 million in 1901. Its resources were taken, the people starved, and the nation was put under debt.

Man has been exploited from the beginning of time. That is the very nature of society – regardless of whether it is affluent or poor. There have also been many attempts at reform, however. Communism was the hope of the world at one time, but the only solution would lie in decentralization of power and control. Decentralization has been tried time and time again but those who bring it into effect then concentrate power into their own hands.

Working with Gianiji I had seen the exploitation both by the British and the maharajahs. Then one came to America because it was the leader of the world. She had the potentials to start a new order based on humanism, not politics or dogmas. So Life brought one to America to see the impact of science on society and to show that humanism is the answer – not reaction or militarism.

In reality there is no America. People came to this continent from different countries of the world, and they met. Some native tribes had lived here for many thousands of years before the others came. The experiment was – how would they relate with each other? Would they share the bounty in this New World?

People came to the New World with hope; it was a step away from Europe's feudalism and the tyranny of religions. But as the world's downtrodden came to this rich land they could not contain themselves. The Gold Rush was as destructive for the white man as alcohol was for the American Indian. As early as 1838, Ralph Waldo Emerson gravely assessed:

"This country has not fulfilled what seemed the reasonable expectation of mankind."

America developed a culture based on seeking external glamour while belittling internal values and principles.

Progress thus offered only increased efficiency. Our education consisted of gaining skills – which allowed us to better compete but we forfeited peace in the process. The law of "might is right" rules in a career-oriented society which always seeks greater competence at gaining advantage for itself. Where man lives by attachment and the unfulfillment of body senses, violence flourishes.

Man, with all his knowledge, is imprisoned in his own world of abstract thought-images. In his quest to train his brain he has neglected and overlooked self-discovery and the spaciousness of serenity. The true purpose of education was to introduce the human being to his vast potentials. We disregard the potential and just train the brain to do routine work like a machine.

We run away from innocence and then need a drink to forget our anxieties. Today every home is crowded with unnecessary things. Simplicity and wisdom are rare; self-forgetfulness has become an absolute necessity.

In America today the small farmer can hardly hold his own against large corporate landowners. And because of his dependence on gasoline and mechanization he does not even have the resources to be self-reliant should gasoline become scarce. We have contaminated the earth and it is becoming almost impossible to restore the necessary balance. We have interfered with just about everything that is natural – food, clothing, animals, and the earth itself.

It is not only in the production of armament that powerful commercial interests ignore consequences for mankind. Some of the policies and practices that increase profits for the food and drug industries in America also increase suffering for the human being.

In his book, *Diet For A New America*, John Robbins states:

> "Our environment and food chains are being inundated by a virtual avalanche of pesticides. What three decades ago took us six years to produce, we now produce every couple of hours.

> "But the very poisonous and persistent qualities of these toxic chemicals have made them big money-makers for the chemical companies who market them aggressively. These corporations have applied enormous political and economic pressure to keep their products in use. The tragic result is that millions of pounds of these lethal agents continue to be used every year." [2]

Citing a National Cancer Institute study, he points out:

> "In 1900, cancer was the tenth leading cause of death in the United States, and was responsible for only three percent of all deaths. Today, it ranks second, and causes

about twenty percent of all deaths. More Americans will die of cancer *this year* than died in World War II, the Korean and the Vietnamese wars combined.

"Forty years ago, cancer in children was a medical rarity. Today, more children die of cancer than from any other cause.

"Many scientists now feel that the presence of toxic chemicals in our bodies is largely responsible for these epidemics." [3]

Democracy or anything else manmade – no matter how good it seems to be – will end up working things to its own advantage. No matter how lofty its beginning, everything degenerates that is of thought and time. Politics, religion, education, and science always follow that law. When you realize this is so, you turn within and say, "I will not work under the authority of another."

Human beings are not important to governments. Whether communistic or capitalistic, their goals are exactly the same – military might and industrial economies. But there is a different way – that way is humanism.

Following World War II the planet was divided into three camps. One was the West – composed of the Americas and Western Europe. Communist countries formed the second group, including the Soviet Union and the Eastern European nations. Finally, about two billion subsistence farmers made up the Third World.

These village dwellers were usually poor, illiterate, and unconcerned with politics.

Most of the world's human energy and resources were in the Third World. These underdeveloped nations had abundant natural resources but needed technological help in order to develop them. Many had been colonies that were exploited by the Western industrialized nations and drained of their natural wealth. A new world order was emerging, and colonies were receiving their independence as the ruling European nations could no longer retain control after the stresses of the second World War.

My survey of America involved making serious inquiry. How would the world's leading nation – America – relate with this mass of human energy, this resource of two billion people? Could she aspire to question the validity of "might is right" and rise to the opportunity of seeing the world as one humanity? Or would her vested interests prevail and focus the nation's economy on military might, leaving the problem of starvation unresolved?

Generations of deprivation had left the Third World with great, crying needs. But it had humanism to offer the West. Over 40,000 leaders of India went to prison while non-violently seeking the country's independence. Some 17,000 women courted imprisonment by breaking unjust British colonial laws that taxed salt, the poor man's necessity. Seventy thousand Indian men protested against the British government in the first Salt March and were sent to jail. Moral issues were of first importance to them.

Mahatma Gandhi said, "We will not correct wrong with over- doing of wrong."

When brought to trial for supporting impoverished peasants, Gandhi said to the magistrate, "The only course open to you is...either to resign your post, or inflict on me the severest penalty, if you believe that the system and law you are assisting to administer are good for the people." Gandhi represented the goodness of humanism. Out of his caring he spoke to what is eternal in man. His was an impersonal action. Gandhi was not interested in politics but in helping end man's misery.

Given that background I was shocked to see that America was bitter about communism, which is only an abstract idea. When confronted with an actual offense, Gandhi could say, "The enemy is not always wrong. I have no personal ill-will against a single administrator, much less can I have any disaffection towards the King's person. But I hold it a virtue to be disaffected towards a Government which in its totality has done more harm to India than any previous system." Wisdom lies in weeding out animosity and becoming objective. Nothing derailed Gandhi's peace. Why should Americans find rising above their own reactions to be so difficult?

Humanism is unchanging – it relates man to what is not of time in himself. Humanism is religious; it offers pure politics, pure skills, and pure intelligence. Humanism is not primitive, for it uplifts the spirit of the planet and introduces man to his higher nature.

The action of humanism was and is needed in this country. But we always tend to think it is the rest of the world that needs something from America. Our industrial power could improve the lot of man, and free him from the drudgery of manual labor. Can America now respect humanism and help the human being on the planet? To do so, we will have to make corrections in our political system.

How many millions of dollars does it take to be elected to office? Anyone who does not have that kind of money is left out. Where is democracy when only a small percentage of people can afford to give expression to their aspiration? Democracy in its pure spirit is humanism. When humanism is absent, there is no democracy.

The lower side of man is of the earth. In the struggle for survival and territory, violence is natural. Militarism predominates when man thinks he is merely of the earth. In actuality he is an eternal spirit, capable of rising to a humane perspective. Nationalism represents the law of might. Nationalism wants more claws and fangs – deadlier weapons. Militarizing the planet may be good for industrial economies, but where is the sanity in it?

There is such wastefulness in wrong thinking, as well as dire consequences. The fact is that only wisdom and rightness are free of consequences. Humanism wants to say, "Listen, that's not the way." And somehow, when I came to this country, I was in contact with that force, and represented it. I had not come to earn money but to volunteer my services. And in this materialistic society I almost starved. Even when the money ran out, I would not compromise and work for another. Self-reliance is an experiment one lived by.

I had wondered if there was space for humanism in the New World. And there was the sense that if it did not go in that direction it would self-destruct. Aldous Huxley said that evil, unable to resist temptation, in the end destroys itself. Being the war's victor nation, the path America chose had an enormous impact on mankind everywhere.

Worldwide overpopulation and illiteracy were two of the many problems after World War II. America's technology could have helped by putting its industrial might and skills to right use. With wisdom, farsightedness, and the spirit of humanism, America could have turned the tide in the world. Had that been done, America would have flourished. But now she will suffer the consequences for having been indifferent to people in sorrow and in need. An opportunity was lost to come to rightness – to discover the spirit of helpfulness and caring – and in doing so, replenish the earth.

CHAPTER SIX

6

AFFLUENCE
WITHOUT WISDOM
IS SELF-DESTRUCTIVE

WISDOM makes one humane. Intellectual learning makes one self-centered. The focus of learning is on improving the personality – which our educational system caters to – while an education of wisdom would introduce us to undoing the primitive and the old within ourselves. Our present education merely extends the tradition of yesterday.

As we become more self-centered there is less space for leisure, wisdom, and peace. Pretty soon we are going the way of consequences because we do not know any other. But we have learned all kinds of ways to *postpone* consequences. If there is a health problem, modern medicine invents injections and pills for dealing with it. And doctors even know the side effects the medicines will have and what to do for those. So nothing ever ends; it just shifts.

Our momentum of learning is an evasion. It does not correct errors, it just tries to hoodwink them.

Self-interest is always present. In India the wise people say that you can not change the basic element of something. You can take gold and make earrings with it. Or you can make a bracelet or rings out of it. You can even smash it up. But it is still gold – the form doesn't matter. Content matters.

Learning is almost always selfish. Focusing on "me and mine" divides man from man, because it is contrary to wholeness. It perpetuates separation and intensifies conflict. Friction and violence continue. And no one wants to cure it even though everyone wants to talk about it. Finally, learning comes up with the notion: "peace through war."

One's first impression of America was that it was clean, efficient, and dependable. Customs officials were not corrupt; nor was the salesman going to try to cheat you. People were healthy and prosperous. Hot and cold water, gas, and electricity all were at your fingertips. Cars and gasoline were inexpensive. One could buy food without worrying about cleanliness, or manufactured goods without being concerned about reliability. Getting on a turnpike, one could not have imagined the efficiency. Even trees were planted along the highway. It was easy to love America.

When you went to the United Nations, what the speaker said immediately was translated into many different languages. One was astonished by what man had accomplished. Even in terms of thoughtfulness America excelled. Meters were in taxis so that passengers would not have to argue with the drivers over fares.

Because the standard of living was high you could trust people. In India if you took your laundry to someone he might tell you to come back for it in a week. But if a wedding took place within the next few days the laundry man might go wearing your shirt.

America was the first nation I had heard of where the government belonged to the people. Government programs helped citizens get homes; the GI Bill helped provide education. This was a friendly government, which is a very rare thing.

But there were also many contradictions: the slums of Harlem and the Statue of Liberty shocked me. Men subject to a constitution are not free – that is a denial of Universal Law. Any civilization that puts the primary needs of man in the second place is unwise. Its thinking is based on false and wrong values. Problems of deprivation in an industrial age are unthinkable from a humanistic point of view. When would America rise to maturity?

Right after World War II Egyptian President Nasser told the U.S. that his country wanted friendship and trade but that it would not provide military bases. "Our war is against poverty," explained President Nasser.

America could have fostered a culture in which goodness was more important than dogma. Without goodness the higher part of man does not surface. Goodness offers harmony and peace, for it demands adherence to different values. It changes the educational system and social life, while keeping the indulgence and outlets of the industrialized world in check. Goodness is good for every nation, and all mankind could contribute. In a regional world of differences, there would be a universal outlook.

Without goodness and harmony the very lure of prosperity deceives man, and leads him to degeneration. America now has an impressive collection of outlets and indulgences, but humanity cannot survive without wisdom and simplicity. Man's brain has invented the finest and most advanced commodities, but the inner man is lonely, afraid, panicky.

> "There are different kinds of poverty. In India some people live and die in hunger. There, even a handful of rice is precious....
>
> "But in the West you have another kind of poverty, spiritual poverty. This is far worse.... You have the poverty of people who are dissatisfied with what they have, who do not know how to suffer, who give in to despair. This poverty of heart is often more difficult to relieve and to defeat. In the West you have many more broken homes, neglected children, and divorce on a huge scale." [1]
>
> MOTHER TERESA

It was shocking to see how nationalism prevents the goodness within from arising, and how affluence becomes a real block in the discovery of man's potential. Sheer affluence does not enrich man. Divorce rates keep going up, and fashions change yearly as though everyone is regulated by someone else.

I watched the United Nations at work. There was no hope for it to succeed. Some of its agencies were beneficial, yes, but it did not fully represent the spirit of humanism. For the most part its interests were nationalistic. The U.N. was dominated by bickering between the two veto-wielding superpowers and would not take bold steps such as limiting the military budgets of all nations. Supposedly, the function of the United Nations was to settle international disputes. There was also the World Court that could have resolved the boundary disputes between the Arabs and the Israelis. But when the superpowers take sides the policy of divide-and-rule prevails. It is a choice between justice and vested interests.

Nationalism is controlled by those who see violence as a solution. And the populace accepts this. Such a country's educational system might be advanced but it will still be primitive in terms of helping man advance. Politicians will speak out against some dictators but become friends with others. "How does that happen?" I wondered. It was like a child who trusts his parents only to find that his faith is unmerited. None of the politicians were statesmen and there were hardly any unbiased voices.

I did encounter a small minority of Americans who were objective. Over the years, however, it became apparent this was insufficient in proportion to the mass of society with lower values. The only way to rise to this nobleness – this goodness – is through the strength of rightness and virtue. But in America, where almost everything is left to manmade rules and to the police, wisdom, simplicity, and non-waste are ignored. The system promotes a belief in tanks and nuclear missiles, not in the power of goodness within each person.

As man loses contact with Eternal Laws, fear intensifies. Today the "best" technology is devoted to destructive means. And it will bring the land to bankruptcy. When a country is strong because it has worked everything in its own favor, will it ever listen to a call for wisdom? America neglected the Navajo, the Hopi, the Cherokee, the Sioux, and others – how is she going to pursue humanism now? Emerson said:

> "One would think from the talk of men that riches and poverty were a great matter; and our civilization mainly respects it. But the Indians say that they do not think the white man, with his brow of care, always toiling, afraid of heat and cold, and keeping within doors, has any advantage of them."

How great a contribution Native Americans could have made had they not been eliminated from the land they had lived in harmony with for tens of thousands of years. Now we lack the wisdom they were to have imparted to the world.

Will America be able to cope with becoming a secondary power? Rampant violence will emerge, and the police will be given even more control.

Immorality is what makes a person inwardly weak. How can any country burn wheat and dump tons of potatoes in the ocean – rather than giving the food to poor nations – in order to protect agricultural prices?

An estimated 40,000 infants die each day in the Third World from nutritional stress and infectious disease. Two billion people today do not have clean water for drinking.

As vast as these problems are, what is spent on just one spaceship or nuclear submarine would go a long way toward protecting human lives. Each day America spends over $3.50 per citizen on defense while about one billion people in the world *live* on one dollar a day. Most of them are under age fifteen, and many will die before reaching age five.

When this country is doing the wrong thing, the fear of communism – or some other "ism" – intensifies. But there is no communism if one is doing the right thing. It is due to lack of humanism that problems arise. Where there is humanism, a nation helps the world build better roads, hospitals, schools, and canals. Would there not be a blessing upon this planet if all of humanity had food to eat,? How could we not be glorified as a nation for doing so?

Humanism is a virtuous way of life. It demands a profound change of values and inner transformation. The world's present system of education, business, and technology has no need for it.

There was great generosity in America after World War II. The Point Four Program and the work of many philanthropic organizations was unprecedented; there was much goodwill. Years before, America had the foresight to grant tax breaks for charitable contributions, and many wealthy families and corporations established foundations, including the Carnegies,

Rockefellers, Ford, and General Motors. They did tremendous good and their administrators were wonderful people. Religious groups such as the Quakers also had extraordinary reputations for their moral character and benevolent work.

But one discovered that the philanthropic expression was not in proportion to the problem. America led the world in such aid but few recognized that philanthropy dealt largely with emergencies. It helped when there were floods, earthquakes, and famines. Afterwards, however, conditions were usually just as they were before the disaster.

What would one have to do in order to be a cause that affects a change? Sustained cooperation and capital in the billions of dollars would be required to create a new wealth in Third World countries. When wells are dug to supply more water, and better seeds and farm equipment introduced, the land starts to produce more crops. Then people have the resources to stand on their own feet at all times. They would be building strength on their own territory rather than becoming dependent on charity.

American industry could have found ample markets in the Third World. This nation would have been no poorer for raising the living standards of other nations. America's integrity could have caused a change of values in the world, bringing an end to the fear and exploitation of another. But the war on communism made government aid more and more subject to politics. Countries which agreed with America, and mostly those that allowed military bases, got the help.

What happened then was that the poor people in the newly-freed colonies got impatient. They became restless when they did not see their situation improving. And one by one governments collapsed in the countries of Asia, Africa, and South America. Rule, for the most part, was taken over by military leadership.

America's global policy was to contain communism, not to harm other countries. Yet when one nation received U.S. military aid, neighboring countries were usually forced to respond in kind. From 1954 to 1963 America spent $1 billion arming and training Pakistani forces. In the face of this growing strength, India was compelled to divert funds meant for the primary needs of man to its military.

Within this country itself, why is there not a Hopi Congressman or Senator? Who represents those people? Is variety encouraged? Is there toleration of differences?

What if there was a real demand that children in schools be taught not to waste? What if Congress passed a law forcing companies which manufacture cans to keep the land litter-free and to recycle the empties? Can America not afford wisdom?

Why are there no laws concerning the violence on television which is perverting children? There is a gun in almost every child's hand. You would think that mothers would protest.

Why is it rare for Americans to take a stand on moral grounds? Is the only time someone stands up when they are asking for higher wages? You do not find thousands of people here going to jail for ethical reasons. And even if a protest march or other event takes place, its effect is limited due to the impact of the mass media. Most of the news is sensational because reporters go to the hospitals and police stations to report on accidents and crime. Every day there are new stories of violence and the public has become immune to shock.

Modern media offers an innumerable variety of distractions. This makes it very difficult to find peace within – or even to find the space which sees the need for peace within.

Children get introduced to these distractions at a young age. This makes it difficult for them to heed the intrinsic call within to their life's real purpose. American democracy offers outlets instead: a circus of choices justified by "I do as I please." Thus, man degenerates, losing his integrity and universality. We are left with pervasive waste and much loneliness.

In an externalized society there is less and less capacity to make contact with the internal, the real. Unless society produces people who can outgrow it by awakening their own potentials, society will remain at a loss.

It is almost impossible today to be free of influences and beliefs. Even though profits and nationalism do not offer freedom, the simplicity of wisdom has little appeal for most people. Pure action of the spirit is snuffed. Is it not worth more than skills and jobs?

CHAPTER SEVEN

7

WHAT IS HUMANISM?

COMMUNISM could not compete with the West after World War II, the Soviet Union alone having lost over 20 million lives and with much of the country in devastation. America's fear could have been avoided through adopting a different approach. If America had used its resources to be the world leader in dealing with problems of human deprivation, how could it ever lack friends?

Humanism would have said, "We do not care what your beliefs and traditions are. America is here to share technology, build better roads, generate electricity, and lead nations to self-reliance. We want to extend goodwill and end poverty and starvation in the world."

Overpopulation, primitive agricultural practices, and poor health care could not be corrected by the Third World. Adequate resources were not available at the national level. Only at the level of humanity could such problems be solved.

I visited the Soviet Union in 1958, and there was not an anti-American feeling there. In America there was hardly a single person who was not contaminated with the suspicion of communism. Communism and capitalism are really no different, for neither produces a change in values. America's superior position was due simply to the fact that her industry and technology were 30 or 40 years ahead of Russia's after World War II. It is probable that Russia's friendship could have been won without superpower competition.

Then what fear was it that drove America to burn its wheat and throw potatoes into the ocean by the tons? One began to see that not only was there paranoia about communism but an insanity that would waste food when there was famine in the world. This fear would at some point destroy America. The divisiveness it has created in the world is also present within, and will become more and more apparent as stresses in society increase.

What is it we have to give that is not of this world? America's political, military, and economic successes will be harmful in the end if their source is wrong-mindedness. One can become weakened even while being externally strong.

Being an extension of humanism at the age of twenty-seven allowed one to come into contact with a handful of superb people who had objective view-points and who made decisions at a high level. In principle they agreed with what I said but there was not much they could do. Although they were Supreme Court Justices and Senators, they were not in charge of America and their voices were not heard. When I met them they explained, "If you have a sane view, you become as if exiled."

No longer are such persons advisers to Cabinet members, for those positions now are political in nature. Today the larger view is not accessible to decision-makers, nor is it reported by the media.

I found that individuals are good, but the system degrades them. The pressure man is under in this technological society will destroy him. As stress increases, morality and ethics deteriorate. That is happening the world over and it is driving man to self-destruction. No one has the space for simplicity.

When I would talk to the Rockefeller Foundation or the leaders behind the Point Four Program, they would say, "You're a good man. You should be ambassador." Then they would suggest someone else for me to go see.

After talking with other people one would go back and say, "I don't want to see anyone else. I've come to see you. What is it that you are willing to do?" Matters would stop there. "Humanism is good – peace is good – but we're in business," would be the answer.

Businesses did not want to invest in Asia. They would refer you to the Red Cross or the Carnegie Foundation for aid. But what the world needed was new wealth. American capital did not want to go to poor countries because it could earn more here. It could make immense profits by manufacturing potato chips or some other unessential goods. Why should it go to Burma? It did not even want to go to Canada. Instead, profits could be gained by increasing publicity here through television, radio – even T-shirts.

America destroys food to obey the laws of commerce since vested interests control the lobbying system and the government. Industry could have developed markets for its goods in the Third World instead of putting more and more human energy and money into the manufacture of arms and the securing of military bases around the world.

Weapons are instruments of destruction while tractors and water pumps produce food and help humanity. Trillions of dollars which we invested in weapons did not in turn produce anything. What an opportunity there was for America to extend reverence for Life, and have the strength of rightness that would ennoble its people. There are consequences for putting energy into destroying life rather than into protecting it. One day we may discover that devoting resources to unproductive armaments leads to bankruptcy. Self-centered economic progress is a form of savagery. It is territorial, and dependent upon "might makes right."

Humanism offers a contact with your own integrity – a different kind of sensitivity which is not personal. It has no prejudice, a condition which nationalism will not allow. It makes no conclusions about another or how a situation should or should not be. For it, what is, is.

Humanism is not schooled. Nor is it a skill, for it is not survival-oriented. Thus it is independent of the physical senses and their illusions. Humanism is not mental. You cannot fit it into the known, for humanism has no beliefs, no conclusions, and no past conditioning. It is the light of attention, free from the seeking of results. Humanism offers a way of life that is free from consequences, for it has no motives.

Humanism is a state of being which is whole and established in itself. It is an unchangeable cause, not an effect. Being related to Life, humanism is natural, free of outside influences and abstract ideas.

Humanism is aware and deals solely with the actual. Those who are with it do not make it a cause, for it can not be organized. Humanism is not an activity or it becomes organized politics or religion. It introduces one to the involuntary, spontaneous action of Life. It is the shared joy of God and goodness with one another.

Humanism awakens the responsibility of being a human being, not a citizen, since Life is divine. It will not fit into conformity, which represents violence and the memory of yesterday. It is the everlasting reality of the present moment, ever new.

Humanism is of awakened awareness, not educated brain cells. It is a vision of the peace and joy of simplicity, independent of educated dogma and institutional beliefs which promote separation.

Man is controlled and pressured by his education to belong to the traditional system's conformity.

Transformation thus is almost impossible, for there is not the Kingdom of Heaven's undivided sacredness in manmade society. There is not the space for the human being to be with his own contentment. Humanism is more valuable than all the education and all the arts in the world. It is what brought one to America.

CHAPTER EIGHT

*Every decision you make
stems from what you think you are,
and represents the value
that you put upon yourself.*

*Believe the little can content you,
and by limiting yourself
you will not be satisfied.
For your function is not little,
and it is only by finding your function
and fulfilling it
that you can escape from littleness.* [1]

8

THE FUTURE
OF MANKIND

Eminent and renowned men and women have talked about non-violence and decentralization. They have warned us about the exploitation and catastrophe resulting from concentration of power in the hands of the few. They have pointed out that with the increase of industrialization and the commercialization of the media, the nations of the world would turn from being a means for the welfare of their people to an end in themselves. A few people have foreseen the consequences of artificial life and the irresponsibility of waste. They appealed to the masses; they had a cause.

Yet the great economists, statesmen, reformers, and scientists have not succeeded in harmonizing and humanizing society. The consequences of affluence and routine life are staring us in the face. The plague of unemployment is upon us, and those who have given their life energy to the artificial and the unessential are now self-spent, faced with their own irresponsibility. Human energy continues to be drained to build industrial economies that thrive on the manufacture of armament. Where is wisdom?

Never in the history of humanity have the instruments of death been so perfected, and so much time and energy allotted to destructive means. Never in history has the efficiency of tax collecting been so thoroughly mastered; nor has the manufacture of artificiality been so commercialized and wasted lives so adored. Never before has educated ignorance been so glorified. Never before has overpopulation gotten so out of hand.

Devoid of wisdom, what is the future of mankind? How few people have their own water to drink. Where is the self-sufficiency of the family or the self-reliance of the individual?

We may well be nearing unemployment of catastrophic proportions. [2] Anything could set it off – an energy crisis, one simple upheaval of earth changes. Even now the slightest economic imbalance can topple the job structure. The economy, monetary system, transportation – no area is truly self- sufficient.

In this complex interdependency, how quickly things could degenerate. Violence and inhumanity could patrol the land. Everyone's life is at stake against the tyranny of hunger, fear, and homelessness.

What will sustain us through the turmoil of the future if today's profit-oriented agricultural systems, electronics, and banking systems – with all their technology – break down? If the system collapses, what do you think it will resort to if not severe taxation? Conformity would become mandatory as a means of control. To cope with lawlessness and disorder, in our horror of scarcity, we would turn against the citizen the vicious means already invented to destroy our so-called enemies. Technology would turn into a god to which we would have to give our life and energy.

With the artificiality of modern life, lack of wisdom the world over has crowded people into cities that hardly produce anything that sustains life. Yet hunger and thirst are ever there, whether supermarkets are open or not. This, one of the most wasteful cultures ever known to history, could overnight be a victim of scarcity.

These are not prophecies or psychic predictions of doom, but realistic observations of industrial and governmental trends.

We thought education would help. Has it? Is man any less conformed? Education, for the most part, provides skills to suit unworthy jobs. Educated for jobs, we are drilled in skills to function in the monetary system of an abstract world. Look how powerfully this abstract culture influences the multitude. Who has a voice of his own or the simplicity of wisdom? Who lives by eternal values?

A sense of helplessness surrounds man today. He is ruled by insecurity and unfulfillment, pressured by time and problems. Man has already lost his own intrinsic work and is subject to a job; thus, he has become false to himself. He has lost the discrimination and wisdom to make his own decisions. He lives by mere choices.

This is the price we are paying for being slaves of gratification and pleasure which know no freedom, only dependence on another. Everywhere in the world it is the same. We have all but lost confidence in ourselves and in our own holiness. Jobs have become important and survival is what we worship. The present misuse of human energy is inconsistent with Higher Laws and will not work.

What God created, He protects. But man, enslaved by profiteering minds, controlled by political systems and corporate monopolies, has moved toward a mercenary civilization. Frustration's need for outlets, and in turn for money, is the universal epidemic. Like a seed, everything extends what it is.

Insecurity is not the issue. Productivity is the issue. True productivity eliminates insecurity. The paradox is that it is our jobs that maintain the insecurity. Today's productivity is linked with the irrelevant. It is the meaningless made essential.

Could you conceive of any culture in the history of mankind that was as concerned with money as we are today? Money is becoming as important as the water we drink and the air we breathe. Therefore, we are subject to someone else's control. Money is in charge and is the dictator of the age. It controls government agencies and most of mankind.

Because of money-making motives, it is not likely that powerful interests – the heads of corporations – will allow peace to exist. The industrial economy does not prosper with peace. It needs war to profit, and human life has become less important than the industrial economy. Henry David Thoreau said:

> "Peace of the world lies not in inventions but in men's hearts and men's souls...to sustain life, we need less rather than more; to protect life, we need courage and integrity, not weapons, not coalitions."

Everything is being taken over by the big industries – the dinosaurs of the modern age. Hate, fear, and vanity are also commercialized by a handful of multitrillionaires who are in charge of the financial and political systems of the world. The whole of humanity suffers, and the gain is only for the few. And this economy is worshipped everywhere!

This is where the meaningless routine of making a living has led us. When we have vested interest and greed, we get exploited. Can you see how decadence is coming into being?

I wish that we could see that the hysteria of self-centeredness and the incessant need to work is not necessary. Then we would learn to afford honesty and would get to know what is of internal value, irrespective of the externals.

How we have deceived ourselves! We seem incapable of being the witness to this movement of external society going towards its self-destruction in the name of progress. There was a time when the human being thought of himself as a human being. Now we are citizens. Citizens belong to some abstract idea or to wars for which they can kill another human being they have never seen before.

Where is humanism?
Where is love?
Where is reverence for Life?
Would the action of love extend hate, war, and prejudice?

In the early part of this century, Swami Vivekananda, a foremost disciple of Sri Ramakrishna, said:

"In the political struggle man must grow continually... He has duties toward his wife, his children, his parents. He has others toward his village, his town, his district, and finally, his country. But all these selfish interests for which he strives so hard are transcended when he becomes a citizen of humanity as a whole, when he sees God Himself in each man he serves. Such a man can move worlds, when his tiny ego is dead and God has taken its place." [3]

Anyone who speaks the truth must point out the insanity of our times and challenge the authority that conforms people. If he cares for you he must point it out to wake you up and bring you to a state that is not deceived.

The issue is irresponsibility. We know conformity; we know duty. We live in a culture where we are told what to do by colleges, by parents, by jobs, by the media. We are indoctrinated and conditioned. How dependent we are. Our knowledge is mostly other people's knowings, nothing direct. These are the appalling discoveries we have to make.

When you are responsible you know no conformity. You are responsible for your life, for your ethics, for your virtue.

A new action has to be born in America. We have to see the detriment that progress has become, but not in America alone. I am talking about what technology has done to man all over the world: he is always pursuing the advantage, always led by wishes. Can we see this, not as a blame but as a fact in itself so that we can come to urgency? Then we are stepping out of the fascination with the external that blossomed here and we turn the tide. We become part of the vibration of the land, of the New World, and we begin to outgrow the externals.

We have to see that century after century everything we have done in the name of progress, in the name of science, in the name of religion, in the name of education, has made us more and more conscious of self-survival. And now we are at the mercy of the system.

See how universally destructive progress has become and be determined not to be a part of it. We must change. Instead of feeling helpless we must find our own potential and relate with other forces rather than with nationalism or manmade laws. The responsibility is ours.

We are who we are because we have limited our-selves to a very small sphere of existence, with its greed and fear, wishing and wanting. Yet life is more than self-survival.

Wherever there is attachment or vested interest we become threatened. And the person we like the least is the one who brings the gift of truth. Such men have rotted in prison, been assassinated, and crucified.

It does not matter where we are in the world the principle is the same: beyond "me and mine" it is difficult for us to go. We are in the bondage of our beliefs. If what you believe is different from what I believe, then there is inevitably a clash.

Can we come to some kind of receptivity knowing that reaction is caused by what we believe? This is where mankind is limited today, as he has been throughout the ages.

More money is spent on armament today than at any time in the whole history of mankind. Countries that cannot afford the luxury of toilet paper maintain armies and sophisticated, deadly weapons. Ours is no longer a war against the capitalist or the socialist; it is a war against the human being.

Wake up!
YOU are the human being!
And you support this tragedy with your prejudices.

Carl Sandburg said there is only one man in the world and his name is All Men. Fear has no nation-ality. Greed, hunger, sex, have no nationality. All men have the same brain. Thinking itself, said Mr. J. Krishnamurti, is common to all men in spite of poverty, illiteracy, sophistication, or affluence. We all think with the same brain.

The technology of computers and mass communications has now advanced to the point of shaping man's very brain and controlling his thinking – almost completely to the advantage of those in control of the system. The horror of this grim fact already at work is perhaps the worst nightmare mankind has ever known. Yet the perversity is hardly visible and we are in danger of being reduced to mere robots. Science now attempts to affect the human species.

Through the control of educational institutions, religious belief systems, political propaganda, and the financial supremacy of vested interests, we are being molded to a sub-human level to function as programmed. As the human brain is being fully manipulated hardly anyone will be able to cope with the ingenious methods of external influence. Man himself, for the first time, is at stake now that the nuclear age with its ultra-modern electronic technology is upon the planet.

With industry's frantic search for consumer markets and the push for military supremacy, the tension amongst nations mounts to explosive points. Violence, greed, and might roam the earth like giant monsters in the guise of corporations and big business. Meanwhile, the New Age commercial "gurus" sell their positive platitudes and cosmic transformations. Man, already in the delirium of nationalism, is not fully aware of what is ahead for the mechanized society.

Heed the words of Mr. J. Krishnamurti spoken at his fifth talk in Saanen, Switzerland, in 1983. He warned that the large corporations of America and Japan are spending billions of dollars developing the fifth generation computer – a mechanical brain of ultra-intelligence – that will be a robot. Twenty-four hours a day the top people of each country are competing with each other to bring about this robot that will outstrip man. This machine is to think faster, create more, do almost everything the human brain has done or can do. This is happening now and for commercial reasons.

What is going to happen to our brains when the computer and robot take over? It will be able to invent the best god on earth, invent better gurus. Man's theories, doctrines, and churches may have no place because the computer will be much more active, much clearer. It will act on the human brain from the outside and bring about a society that will function mechanically.

Mr. Krishnamurti continued by saying that if we, as human beings, do not change from within ourselves we are going to be changed from the outside. This is inevitable and very, very serious.

Hear also the words of Mr. R. Buckminster Fuller as he speaks of the power of *The Grunch Of Giants*:

"There is no dictionary word for an array of invisible giants, one thousand miles tall, with their arms interlinked, girding the planet Earth. Since there exists just such an invisible, abstract, legal-contrivance array of giants, we have invented the word GRUNCH as the group designation – a 'grunch of giants.' GR-UN-C-H, which stands for annual GROSS UNIVERSE CASH HEIST, pays annual dividends of over one trillion U.S. dollars....

"GRUNCH'S giants average thirty-four years of age, most having grown out of what Eisenhower called the post-World War II 'military-industrial complex.' The grunch of giants consists of the corporately inter-locked owners of a vast invisible empire, which includes airwaves and satellites; plus a vast visible empire, which includes all the only eighteen-year-old and younger sky-scraper cluster cities around the world, as well as the factories and research labora-tories remotely ringing the old cities and all the oriental industrial deployment, such as in Taiwan, South Korea, Malaysia, Hong Kong and Singapore. It controls the financial means of initiating any world-magnitude mass-production and -distribution ventures. By making pregraduation contracts with almost all promising university science students, it monopolizes all the special theoretical know-how to exploit its vast inventory of already acquired invisible know-how technology....

"Who runs GRUNCH? Nobody knows. It controls the world's banks. Even the muted Swiss banks. It does what its lawyers tell it to. It maintains technical legality and is prepared to prove it. Its law firm is named Machiavelli, Machiavelli, Atoms & Oil. Some think the second Mach is a cover for Mafia....

"GRUNCH didn't invent the Universe. It didn't invent anything. It monopolizes know-where and know-how but is devoid of know-why. It is preoccupied with absolute selfishness and its guaranteed gratifications. It is as blind as its Swiss banks are mute....

"While the giant now owns and controls four-fifths of the planet Earth's open market bankable assets, one trillion dollars of those giants' assets are in monetary gold bullion....

"The Grunch of Giants – the supernational corporate conglomerates – [are] the greatest giants in all history invisibly 'rough riding' planet Earth. While you can see their skyscrapers and factories, these are only the physical properties occupied by the human-drone workers employed by the elusively invisible corporate conglomerates...." [4]

As violence, distrust, decadence, panic, and the craze for armament increase, life on the planet is affected. Where each person is limited to his own vested interest, the outcome of flourishing self-centeredness will surely lead to consequences.

In Third World countries, the population explosion is most rampant and least controlled because there is not much they can do. Even if their gross national revenue were spent on population control – at the cost or neglect of agricultural projects and other necessities of life – it would not be in proportion to the problem. Sufficient resources at the national level are not available.

It is a human problem, however, not a national one. The resources at the human level are adequate, though mankind lacks the humanism to employ them. The problems that remain unresolved result in devastating consequences.

Politics and religion, which are beginning to compete for supremacy, are also becoming dependent on the invisible bosses who are in control of the monetary system of the world. The cost of elections is so high that in most cases the candidates have become subject to the control of those in charge – for the simple reason that for them to come to prominence requires big money.

Behold the profile of our times!

The question is, can humanity be helped externally? Society is not apt to change; but it is still possible for the individual to come to an inner transformation. The only possible transformation is change within the individual. To settle for personal survival or advantage is not sufficient.

Where, then, is the gratefulness that inspires man and brings him to the action of the soul – the indefatigable spirit of creation? Do you not see that man is tired without the energy of love and his contact with God? Would you not like to be free from the preoccupation of fear and insecurity, and the torment of conflict within and without?

As long as man has lived he has tried to avoid wars and thereby maintained them. If our interest is truly in avoiding war we will end the conflict in ourselves, for that is where it springs from. External war merely manifests what is there in each person. As long as we have reactions, likes, and dislikes, there will be war. It is as simple as that.

So, how do we end war? We end it within ourselves. Coming to peace within is the ending of war.

> "The true glory is reserved not for the man who can throw a bomb, but for him who can stand up and say, 'I possess nothing but God.'" [5]

Our basic problem is that we do not heed what the wise has to say. It is all there. And obvious too. But we remain caught in the misperceptions of our own knowing and irresponsibility remains the statement of our lives.

We have to reverse our dependence on the externals so as not to rely solely on the body senses. This is the step we have to take. And yet so few have taken a step beyond the physical senses. Joy is in the humility of a modest life not driven by unfulfillment.

Contemporary man has such little knowing of Divine Laws, hardly any relationship with truth and peace of mind, or contact with his own inner resources. His vast potentials remain unexplored. How few the world over are the men who are not ruled by the external, who love one another, and who yearn for the sanity of righteousness.

The wise person sees that "me and mine" has no existence in reality. He sees the deception of ideas, that they are abstract; the illusion of the future, that it is self-projected. He sees the fallacy of accomplishment, that it projects future fears and violates the purity of trust in the spirit.

We are so afraid to trust in virtue and to see the good in a brother. Love and thoughtfulness are related to Heaven, to laws that govern the universe. When man has learned to give, he is in charge of the very planetary system.

To know the truth of Love and to extend it is the challenge each individual has to face. It is not the changing of an opinion or a concept; it requires an internal correction. Trapped in the illusions of his own physical senses, mankind as a whole has avoided this action throughout the centuries.

The virtuous action of "LOVE YE ONE ANOTHER" will survive the failure of economy or any other disaster. For when we start with giving we are productive out of the abundance of a just life. The action of our care for the brother is complete unto itself. To Grace, external scarcity is not a fact. We need to be a strength to another and this is achieved by the mastery of life within.

We have the resources and the capacity to change. No matter what our individual situations are, all that is required is our pure intent. No one need be pressured into helplessness. Change is an internal action that starts with self.

Therefore, will you resort to the expedience of the system or will you live according to your own conviction?

Out of this chaotic environment and the insanity of our times, with its tremendous capacity to abuse human energy and the energy of nature, is given the self-reliant action of *A Course In Miracles*. It helps us discover that survival is not the goal of life, salvation is. Man has searched and yearned for lifetimes for the keys inherent in *A Course In Miracles*; saints and prophets have tried to give us a glimpse of the glory and splendor of a thought-free state. Now the Course has come with its step-by-step curriculum and, with it, the light to awaken us to awareness.

A Course in Miracles states most encouragingly:

"In my defenselessness my safety lies."

You who feel threatened by this changing world, its twists of fortune and its bitter jests, its brief relationships and all the "gifts" it merely lends to take away again; attend this lesson well. The world provides no safety. It is rooted in attack, and all its "gifts" of seeming safety are illusory deceptions. It attacks, and then attacks again. No peace of mind is possible where danger threatens thus.

The world gives rise but to defensiveness. For threat brings anger, anger makes attack seem reasonable, honestly provoked, and righteous in the name of self-defense....

Defenselessness is strength. It testifies to recognition of the Christ in you. Perhaps you will recall...that choice is always made between Christ's strength and your own weakness, seen apart from Him. Defense-lessness can never be attacked, because it recognizes strength so great attack is folly.... And in defenselessness we stand secure, serenely certain of our safety.... For you will know that Heaven goes with you. [6]

Man is of divine origin. When we undermine that, we undervalue the action of Life itself.

When man is transformed,
the world is affected.

He is
the whole,
the totality of the universe.

CHAPTER NINE

The memory of God comes to the quiet mind.
It cannot come where there is conflict,
for a mind at war against itself
remembers not eternal gentleness.

The means of war are not the means of peace,
and what the warlike would remember
is not love.

War is impossible
unless belief in victory is cherished.
Conflict within you must imply
that you believe
the ego has the power to be victorious. [1]

9

WHY
HAS THERE ALWAYS BEEN
WAR IN THE WORLD?

WE CAN ALWAYS find factors for war: industrial economy, border disputes, overpopulation, religion, and so forth. but it is imperative that we understand *why* there is war, *why* there is the energy of friction, *why* there is conflict within man. We are talking about some inherent part of man's nature that resorts to war, that makes it take place.

In order to comprehend why there has always been war, it is necessary to understand the nature of the planet and its different levels. Creation itself is beautiful. Yet as it gets more and more engrossed in the energy of the earth it becomes more and more aggressive and, therefore, isolated. In this earth energy, with its instinct for survival, there is fear and competition. The earth produces trees that compete for sunshine, certain creepers that take over everything. It produces animals that kill each other.

For the causes of war, then, rather than looking at individual incidents of war, we should observe the characteristics of earth energies themselves.

What the earth produces is competitive and wants to dominate. Competition is violence. Therefore, violence is inherent in the earth. That is the nature of the earth. And as long as man gets his body from the earth, inherent in that body is that quality of violence. As long as man's consciousness is consistent with the energies of the earth, he also produces those vibrations upon the earth. We can see how natural it is for armament to come into being. We have weapons that could destroy all of humanity and "might makes right."

Earth energies are violent by nature. We see it within ourselves: there is violence; there is jealousy; there is attachment; there is anger. What we know are earth energies with their cravings, wantings, and fears. Look at all the billboards, the ads, the movies, the media. See what is happening everywhere in the world – lives lived in a circus of activity. But can it be a substitute for reality?

What, then, is our function on the earth? We are to awaken to that which is not of the earth, to bring the Kingdom of God so that we can change the vibrations of the earth. The body is only the means of bringing the Kingdom of God to earth in order to transform the vibrations here. Without this transformation we remain part of earth energies, ruled by the body, inherent in which is violence.

Violence increases more and more because we are less in contact with our eternity. In this process, then, of isolation from reality, we use the energy of the earth. The impact of earth energies is strong on all of us. We know but the energy of friction for the most part. Ambition is the energy of friction. Anger and attachment are the energy of friction. Desire is the energy of friction.

We must change our whole concept of who we are. We cannot know peace through our three dimensional faculties; we have to outgrow them. The earth needs our peace. We came to this plane to affect the forces of the earth, not to get caught in the bondage of the body and time. We are the altar of God upon the earth. And we, whom the earth supports and sustains and nourishes, are not doing our job. We have an essential function and we are interfering by not bringing these other vibrations.

Earth energy always wants. Even in its giving it always wants. When we learn to give as we have received, that is when we will experience love for our brothers. Then we are part of wisdom and bring sanity to earth energy, freeing man from his cravings, his fears, his lusts and destructiveness.

Energy must express itself. What we express is a matter of decision. For us to remain indifferent is merely a statement that we have chosen to express earth energies which are warlike. Each person is responsible for war. Therefore, we cannot blame other people for we, too, are part of the energy of the earth. And as long as we live by earth energies wars are inevitable.

We have become children of earth forces – timebound and self-centered. Man, like bodybound animals and plants, has a tremendous urge for survival. And earth energies are now isolating us further and further. We have all but forgotten what relationship is. Now we have dependency. And at the level of dependence we have preferences, all limited to body sensations. Relationship has been replaced by our grouping together at the level of ideas such as communism, socialism, and nationalism.

Characteristically, earth energies thrive on friction. The earth is fragmented into countries and there are always border disputes. Friction comes when there is fragmentation. There can be no friction where there is wholeness.

What causes fragmentation? What binds us to different social groups? Doubt. We doubt everything. First of all, we doubt ourselves. We do not believe we are loved by God or that He created us in His Image. We do not believe that Love is stronger than all else, that innocence is superior to educated ignorance.

Points of view do not relate with truth. Where there is doubt there is no truth; there is fear. Where there is anger there is no love. Yet any man who can turn his cheek has saved a whole nation. A man who cannot hurt another, who will not justify his anger or his hate, would bring an end to the arms race.

We see "In God We Trust" on every dollar bill. Do you think that a nation that trusted in God would trust in armament? We cannot have it both ways.

Where is the human being who stands taller than the stars and the sky because he is virtuous? His very being upon the planet is a blessing and a light.

It requires being responsible and honest. And we must begin with ourselves. We will soon discover how conditioned we are, how indoctrinated we are. Concepts, ideas, and fear are all earth-born. And all these external influences have molded us into a different way of thinking.

In the human being the destructive energy of the earth works through thought. All fear and insecurity are of thought. Thought knows nothing other than fragmentation. And in fragmentation are preferences, choices, projections, and desires – the diseases in which we are caught.

If we understood this we could no longer belong to any man-made dogma that further fragments. We would no longer depend on so-called social forces that fragment under the illusion of promoting harmony. They merely represent aggression. If there were harmony we would never belong to anything that is concerned with survival, for it would not be necessary.

There is a difference between humanity and society. Humanity, or humanism, relates with Eternal Laws. When we are part of society we relate with relative knowledge. Relative knowledge means that we can doubt one minute and believe the next; we can like this and dislike that. It is always relative. There is a constant struggle within and it is ever uncertain. It can become fanatic, but it cannot be certain of fact.

Society can be stimulated and led to embrace dogmas and belief systems. And we are caught in our nationalistic views, our religious prejudices. We have other people making decisions for us. The result is rather sad. We have become duty-bound because we are irresponsible for our own lives.

To observe this is not to react to it. Observation is not contaminated with a point of view. Real observation has no animosity, no judgment, no ill feelings. It just observes and is untouched by bias and judgment. Observation deals with fact. To be with the fact is to end conflict, and then harness its strength of non-duality. Opinions and judgment promote fanaticism at best, whereas the fact is something we experience when we are outside of duality.

A fact relates us to humanity. Fact cannot be taught. It is something one realizes. So then, how do we come into contact with a fact? Certainly not in schools because there we simply acquire skills to make a living. Schooling serves our sense of insecurity, the sense of survival. It is a form of conformity.

What, then, is a fact?

A fact does not change. A fact is something that relates us with eternity, something outside of time. "In God We Trust" is a fact and applies to humanity; it deals with mankind all over the world and for every generation yet unborn.

Fact transforms a person who then steps out of the values of society and relates with eternal values. He is not against society, but a light in society. It is a transformation that takes place within. And then he contributes to all humanity not just to society.

> *As Heaven's peace and joy intensify when you accept them as God's gift to you, so does the joy of your Creator grow when you accept His joy and peace as yours. True giving is creation. It extends the limitless to the unlimited, eternity to timelessness, and love unto itself. It adds to all that is complete already, not in simple terms of adding more, for that implies that it was less before. It adds by letting what cannot contain itself fulfill its aim of giving everything it has away, securing it forever for itself.*

> *Today accept God's peace and joy as yours. Let Him complete Himself as He defines completion. You will understand that what completes Him must complete His Son as well. He cannot give through loss. No more can you. Receive His gift of joy and peace today, and He will thank you for your gift to Him.* [2]

Deep within each person there abides that faith in himself even though it has been forgotten in the mania for progress. And the disease is spreading all over the world – more and more activity that robs us of our real nature.

The man at peace is the one who represents humanity. To him each person is a human being irrespective of skin color, irrespective even of his point of view. How little we know of what does not separate itself.

At the level of wisdom there is no fragmentation because there are no opposites. There is only One Life and the relationship within that Life of which we are all a part. Jesus said, "LOVE YOUR ENEMIES." [3] Mahatma Gandhi said, "The enemy is not always wrong." Unless we come to wholeness, where we have transcended earth energy, fragmentation and friction will not leave us alone.

What constitutes wisdom? Wisdom is the knowledge that you are blessed. Once you know that, your whole perspective changes and you represent God on earth. We are capable of loving all things, for all things are of God. Therefore, you are never touched by insecurity or fear or hate for another person, irrespective of what they do.

Wisdom relates with that which is of God's creation. It has something to give. Wisdom has the ability to act without the fear of consequences – you are your own person extending your own conviction, having your own feet on the ground. You are independent. Free – not of government – but of fear and vested interest within yourself. And you have a voice.

When the body starts to express wisdom, that body then knows serenity. When it is not expressing heavenly energy it is caught in its friction, fragmentation, worry, anxiety, the division of a "you" and a "me."

Our job is to see the friction and limitations of earth energy and come to an awareness that is independent of the earth, where you and I become extensions of Life, and there is no "you" or "me."

How many generations upon generations have been deceived. We are not making right use of the earth or of our bodies. We are abusing everything including our own selves. We cannot make right use of the body if we harbor ambition or fear. In the absence of a new awareness we remain what we are – self-centered and fascinated with accumulation and advantage.

See the tendencies of earth energies. They are craving, competitive, unfulfilled, ever wanting more. The body has choices; and those choices rule the body. When we are in the service of the body, we need jobs. Everyone is educated. For what? To work for those who have control over material existence and authority over men's lives. We are part of a mercenary society where we are drugged into jobs and sell our liberty for money, our energy sapped by routine work. Self-survival has become deeply ingrained and has become synonymous with jobs. But it does not invoke a yearning for the higher values of Life.

Do you not see the mediocrity of man so limited? What do we know beyond physicality and borrowed phraseology? If we lack wisdom, what will our values be?

Helpless people are easy to harness by those who live by advantage. Plants want to get to the sun, man wants to get to the point of advantage. There is no love in it. Nations do the same thing.

If we understand the nature of earth energies we cannot condemn anyone, for we share the same characteristics of that level of existence. Yet we are far more than that. We are as God created us, unchanged by the changeable society that rules our body with its belief systems.

That is the tragic part, that we do not yearn to discover who we are – eternal beings. What good is all our education or religion if we have not discovered the reality of who we are? When we know only our physicality, we build a disastrous world.

Earth energies promote activity. Earth energy that knows only activity is devoid of wisdom. Without wisdom it destroys itself. And so each nation strives for superior weapons. Do you not see what mankind is doing? See how activity is spreading all over the world: faster, quicker, endless. Do you not see the nightmare of it? Where is serenity or peace? Activity has just added greater efficiency to destruction.

We then have to work in order to pay the rent, to buy food, to entertain ourselves in order to bear the routine of uncreative life. Distractions and violence are rampant. We do not recognize who we are; we know only what we have been shaped and molded and programmed to be.

What does our activity accomplish? More artificiality? More cans and litter on the streets?

Deprived of happiness, which is within, we go for pleasure and abuse ourselves or someone else.

Wisdom is not of the earth. It is of Heaven and it puts an end to activity. At the activity level, there are always consequences. We can go on improving transportation, the media, manufacturing, and armament, but the fact remains that activity bears consequences because it cannot be still.

Accumulate this, destroy that. This is what the earth forces have wrought in man. For it is man who destroys; it is man who is the deadliest of all and the most primitive of creatures. Yet he is also the highest and the noblest.

We need desperately to produce men who are not of the earth. Christ said: "THAT WHICH IS BORN OF THE FLESH IS FLESH; AND THAT WHICH IS BORN OF THE SPIRIT IS SPIRIT." [4] Spirit is never contaminated. It is as pure as the Will of God. God created the spirit and the Son of God is spirit.

The minute we are identified with the body or with the earth or with the world of opinions, my body hates you and your body is suspicious of me; and I make money by having your body work for me. Earth energies are at work with all their cravings, wantings, projections; all their efficiency, technology, wars.

We are primitive people well-dressed. We are traders and businessmen; we trade and sell our body energies. We are owned. What do you think we are going to produce? When we do not know happiness, out of sadness and fatigue and frustration, what are we going to do? What kind of world will we produce? Can you see the insensitivity with which we live? Who is happy?

Then there are men like Gandhi who can say that he would die but he would not kill. That is not the voice of earth energies.

Gandhi's stand must bring us to crisis, to the integrity to say, "I can no longer live this way." But where is the energy we need to come to crisis? We either submit to earth energies or we become helpless. Neither is appropriate. What is fitting is to see the fact of it.

Seeing the fact makes it unbearable to live contrary to what our real nature is. Our real nature is not of the earth because we are the Son of God. Even if we cannot understand this we must be determined to give all we have to finding out for ourselves, for we are miserable without knowing the truth of it.

Where is that passion for truth, for God – another purity, another vibration that does not have the physicality of compromise and failure? "THY WILL BE DONE IN EARTH, AS IT IS IN HEAVEN." [5] There is within each person the memory of God. God is that which precedes creation. Awareness is the light in which there is no separation and no form. In awareness we are much bigger than that which is manifest.

We have all compromised, and therefore, we have low opinions of ourselves. We find safety in withdrawing and are left with very little confidence. Confidence is born out of passion. This is not the passion of sexuality. Passion is not for things. Ambition is for things, for status, for lust. Passion has no opposite. It is a fire.

Our knowing only knows how to continue the aggressive, assertive, violent action of earth energies. Real knowing would mean that we are free of it. It would bring us to the energy of silence. We know either one or the other; there is no in-between.

We live by the energy of friction and are oblivious to what pure energy is. When we live by pure energy, who is going to dominate us and who is going to tell us what to do?

If we really saw that the only energy we know is that of friction, the truth of it would silence us. Silence is the pure energy we are speaking of, the energy that inspires us into a different state of gladness. That is the pristine energy – the purest.

Energies contained rise to wisdom. They have conquered unfulfillment and, in wisdom, man is free. Unfulfillment merely exploits earth energies and in that exploitation it murders or kills anyone who stands in its way; everything is abused and commercialized – be it man or nature.

We are still part of the earth energies when we are drawing attention to ourselves and want to impress other people; we are in the bondage of the self. Insecurity is part of earth energies. Insecure people invariably want to impress others, and thus they have a false livelihood and profession.

Begin to see what society does. The system has a routine and we no longer think love or truth are necessary. All we need is affiliation with the tribe. Nationalism becomes necessary – whether it be American, Russian, Chinese, Canadian, or Mexican.

Knowing this, we could not be taken over by nationalistic propaganda. Truth would keep us liberated from the influence of earth forces. We are protected when we know truth, for truth is not affected by earth energies. Our eternal holiness is unaffected by what is external to it. Our eternal holiness is what we need to extend; this is our original purpose. Something else begins to unfold when we see the whole rather than fragmentation. The unfolding of it takes place within us.

We can see the pattern of earth energies, how they work: greed enslaves us, worry preoccupies us; there is the law of punishment and reward. And out of these are born preferences and choices. We remain related to pressures and circumstances – what is favorable to me, what is unfavorable to me. There is no freedom in it. We begin to worship status and privileges: he is so and so because he has palaces or he owns a big corporation or he is a senator or he is a cook. Yet no human being is any less than another.

It is not so much what a person does; we must try to discover what a person is. The more blind we are to man's reality, the more we create an external world in which disharmony and the energy of friction predominate. How much money do you think nations are spending on friction? How much to keep it alive with daily propaganda?

Millions of lives could be destroyed by nuclear bombs. Have you ever thought that the root of it is that we live by the energy of friction, that this is what stimulates us rather than thoughts of peace?

Can we come to the energy of love that wants to share rather than to defend? Can we come to harmony rather than perpetuate the energy of friction? Why introduce the energy of friction into our lives?

It takes wisdom to recognize the situation. And that is probably the one thing we thought the affluent world could do without. Of course, we can do without it if we love destruction, especially self-destruction. The more earthy people are, the more violent. Earth energy is very prevalent where we create sophisticated weapons. Anywhere we are confined to the intellect, rather than related to ethics and nobleness, is a breeding ground for earth energies. Yet the New World is somehow aching to flower into new consciousness.

So, truth is necessary; love is necessary; something that is not of the earth is necessary. "THOU SHALT NOT KILL" becomes truly meaningful. "LOVE YE ONE ANOTHER" becomes a declaration of freedom from earth energies. Where everything is sheltered by the blessing of God, how can there be war?

The minute you are free of earth energies you are giving to the world something it has been waiting for. There is a relationship then. The earth provides the food and shelter, and you provide it with the truth, the light – different vibrations. Then you can never be insecure, for you have the earth as your friend. Seeking ends and the knowledge of love comes. There is love where there was fear. Your presence upon the planet has a powerful impact. It affects the very thought system of man all over the world.

Do you not see what an opportunity we have? Instead of bringing fear and hate and tension into the world, we can bless it. As a human being, as one who has that eternal holiness within, you have a responsibility. And the Will of God will help. Having heard this you owe it to yourself to bring a change in your life. All the potentials are within you to do so. You have already been helped by the recognition of the fact. Recognition of a truth takes no time.

We have accomplished everything in our lives through struggle and effort, by holding on and putting things under lock and key. It has seemed to take a long time because we were always going towards time. We have used time to deviate into, to wallow in with wishing and wanting. It is now very difficult for us to accept that something can be achieved without effort. But to end time we do not need time. This is the mercy of God.

It is our responsibility, our decision, to find out what our choices are all about. They are either based on fear or on love. There is no in-between. In love there is no separation between you and your brother. Somewhere you make a deliberate decision to love your brother more than yourself, and the interests of another become more important than your own.

No one can give what he has not received. It is only in the giving that we will receive, thereby establishing a new relationship, not with the earth, but with Heaven.

When we have love for one another, we are a strength to each other – a moral strength to overcome the energies of the earth. When man becomes selfless, bigger than his vested interest, he has something to give. Mother Teresa has something to give. To those who have the capacity to receive, the Given is always accessible. They outgrow jobs. They outgrow insecurity. They outgrow nationalism. They come to the beauty, the holiness, and the sacredness that is within them. To live a life according to Eternal Laws is to be awakened within.

So, do not look for wise people outside of yourself. Every single person has the potential. The Kingdom of timelessness is found within yourself. Having found it, something else is upon the planet. That something else – call it awareness – is not subject to the laws of the earth with its fears and insecurity. Having outgrown everything of survival and the accumulative process, your awareness has no wishes or wantings. Fulfillment is the fruit of desirelessness and the joy of having something to give.

And then the planet itself and everything upon it receives it too. You are a unique being and angels hover around you.

Life is holy and so are we. We are children of love and truth. We are part of eternity. Let us not limit ourselves to earth energies.

Let us but go towards our eternity,
and all the forces of the universe
will be there to help us.

CHAPTER TEN

Let us be still an instant,
and forget all things we ever learned,
all thoughts we had,
and every preconception that we hold
of what things mean and what their purpose is.

Let us remember not our own ideas
of what the world is for.
We do not know.
Let every image held of everyone
be loosened from our minds
and swept away. [1]

10

THE NEW AGE

THERE IS a general feeling in this part
of the world that we are in the midst of a "New Age"
movement. We tend to think of "New Age" as
something new, of today. Yet there has never been a
time when there was not a new age. When man
discovered fire, it was new; when he discovered the
wheel, it was new; when he discovered electricity, it
was also new.

More important than external discoveries is the
inner discovery of one's relationship with oneself and
with all that is. It is an internal relationship that
bridges the gap of separation between man and
nature, between man and man, between man and
God. And the New Age is meant to bring a person to
that inner unity.

Before we go any further it would be good to see
how words have lost their meaning. It is difficult to

communicate with people because everybody "knows." Today our very knowing – actually educated ignorance – has become our problem. We seldom hear what is being shared because we have already defined in our minds what is being communicated; we have our interpretation.

Listening is an act in which the mind comes to stillness for a moment. Something creative takes place that was unknown before – a new energy, a new clarity. The still small voice within is heard and when that takes place it is bigger than the self, though it takes place within the self. One such moment makes a person humble, makes one loving, makes one appreciate truth. When you discover that, you add a quality to your life and to the lives of others.

Who listens that way? Our excessive learning prevents listening, prevents the new; and in this way it has become detrimental. For external things, we need the senses and we need to learn. But somewhere there must come a time when the senses are stilled and another action takes place that brings discovery.

To me, this is the "New Age": the discovery within me that I am not separated from anything in the world. It ends dependence on external organizations, for it is a miracle that takes place within. And then relationship comes into being. In relationship there is no separation because it is an expression of the One Life.

Our knowing prevents relationship because we are unfulfilled, insecure, worshipful of ambition, and certain that "we" are going to do it. We can become very self-convinced. Yet it takes more than having a sincere motivation to make something work.

We have to question – not out of fear and not out of reaction – but to question with an honesty and a vitality that words alone cannot represent. This would bring us to overcoming all that is of thought. In the questioning is the introduction of humility. For the first time, *you* do not know.

In that moment there is an electric perception. Something else takes place. We establish a relationship with the Unknown, with what is boundless. It is accessible to all, whether it be Einstein, a great poet, a statesman, a housewife, you, or me. We change human consciousness every time we touch upon such clarity.

Let us call the "New Age" the living moment. Can we come to the living moment and its vitality, its wisdom and love, its care for man? In that living moment of the present man rises to the height of his being. And whatever he does has a blessing and sacredness to it. It begins to grow and it can know no failure.

The "New Age" that we know, however, is but a trend: people meditating, burning incense, going to health food stores, becoming healers, so forth. The trend will one day disappear because another trend will take its place.

Let us look at what the mind of the age is, for it is influenced by the current trends. Never on this planet has man been so fatigued and depleted. As a result, outlets have become of major importance. We must look at these things. In what way is our New Age bringing stillness and relaxation, not through drugs, but through some real inner comprehension of who one is?

Beingness is something of eternity. It does not get caught in circumstances. It does not do things to suit the trends. It is independent of it all and that is why it cannot be affected by anything external.

When we do something that is not creative, that is not an expression of our being, but only an expression of our ideas and our brain, life becomes dull. We then need beer, cigarettes, potato chips, cinemas, newspapers, and so forth.

When we talk about the world getting worse, we are saying that we cannot depend on the external world, that it is a sinking ship. If we know it is a sinking ship we do something about it. But the tendency is for us not to hear, or to hear and forget. Nothing lasts, no matter how big the commotion.

Out of all this commotion many young people get involved in sexuality and drugs. More destruction of morality. We cannot ignore that. In what way has the New Age movement brought about moral strength, the standing up for a principle by which one would live no matter what the circumstances?

It is each person's responsibility to find out whether there is any validity to moral strength. New Age leaders flourish where people have not given thought to it. But what is new about their own lives? Are new ethics more prevalent?

Jesus came and there was something new. He did not have a church; He did not hire labor to build one; and He never charged money. That was new. Have you known anyone like that? Then what is new?

Trends come and go. I would call "trends" the old age, not the new. The old is based on time, on "me and mine." And the new is to be related to eternity. That is its difference.

Trends have fascinated many people. At one point non-violence was introduced and many people participated in strikes based on human issues. Today, strikes are prevalent where labor unions bargain for profit, but hardly ever for some moral principle. What does that say to you? That people are complacent? That on moral issues we seldom take a stand?

The New Age can exist where there is respect for a person who stands for some ethic. It would require some sacrifice, some renunciation, some integrity. Where are the leaders today who live by these?

Let us, for instance, look at the recent history of India. The freedom of India came, due to Gandhi and many thousands of other men who had gone to prison because they stood for some conviction, some idea for which they could sacrifice everything – men of ethics and integrity. They had some moral principle by which they lived, some standard. They discovered the principle of non-violence and brought that to application. That was new. Tolstoy had spoken of it; Ruskin had spoken of it; Thoreau had spoken of it; as had the ancient scriptures. But it had not been brought to application at the collective level.

The freedom of India from Great Britain was achieved peacefully. This is quite a historical event because those who rule a nation do not necessarily want to leave when the situation is profitable. And those who revolt usually resort to some form of violence and war ensues as a result of "might is right."

And so, non-violence caught fire. It was felt to be a great contribution to all of mankind because now the way was being paved to settle issues through the means of non-violence. Throughout the world non-violence was spoken of as "new" – a New Age.

Where is non-violence today? There is more armament than mankind has ever known. Do governments listen to protests anymore? Where is the New Age and the betterment it was meant to bring? When the media controls people, we are made more helpless than ever. In that sense, I would say the degeneration – the decline in morality and ethics – is far greater.

Since the end of the Second World War, tension, insecurity, and fear have increased measurably, as has the propaganda against the "enemy." And that is the New Age?

Be aware! Belief in the New Age is more prevalent than the actuality of the New Age.

If the New Age were a fact, we would have greater freedom. There would be greater peace both in our lives and externally. Governments would not be spending so much money on armament and defense systems. We would have more leisure and would be waking up within, finding our own resources rather than becoming more dependent on stimulation, pleasure, and liquor. The increase in tension and outlets is more prominent today than ever. And then we become dependent on the indulgence that society promotes – all kinds of outlets so that we can escape from our own inner poverty.

It is necessary to have a broad view of the state of the world. We can see that there is a proliferation of armament, humanity is more controlled, we have a perverted value system, and real democracy is on the decline.

Today, the United States government is gripped by a tremendous deficit. Someone has to pay that debt. How did it come about if not through irresponsibility and lack of wisdom? Why would we allow a government to be under debt? And that is the New Age? Do you realize how many generations it will take to pay such a deficit? Can you see the consequences it is going to bring and how much suffering it is going to cause to all of humanity? Do you think you are going to escape its consequences? Is this the New Age – people talking about betterment when the facts are otherwise?

How would you look at it if you were humanistic? How do you look at it as a citizen?

May we begin by just seeing the fact? Awaken yourself and find out. Where is most of the national income spent? On armament? Or does it go toward the human being, for his comfort, his betterment? Is there more concern about those who have less in the world? Are we beginning to function as one humanity or are we still with the opportunistic attitude that "me and mine" comes first, both at the national level and at the individual level? In this New Age, is "me and mine" any less dominant?

Within national boundaries we create these biased views and prejudices. But at the human level there is only the human being. Yet we have enough weapons to destroy the world many times over. And in the building of that kind of defense system we have become morally weak and corrupt for the most part. The danger to this country may well be the collapse from within the nation rather than the threat from outside forces.

We could say that there does seem to be progress from the standpoint of our scientific and technological achievements. But to what ends? What are they used for primarily? The finest scientists – what are they producing? Nuclear weapons? Missiles? Only a portion of their energy goes towards some need of humanity. When we put most of our energy into defense, the abuse of science is probably greatest. Has man not betrayed science?

What does education consist of in this New Age? Does it awaken in the student his greater potentials to be more humane? Or is it to prepare him to fit into a job, thereby stamping insecurity permanently on humanity?

Is money the most important factor in the New Age? Is this the New Age, where money and governments control the human being more than ever before;

where man has all but lost the liberty of making his own decisions; where he has become duty-bound and irresponsible at the same time? We worship helplessness. And helplessness is drawn to its opposite: to power and to might.

What would bring about a transformation in us today? Do we have inner strength or would we stay true to the idea that we are helpless? Could we stand on our own conviction? It is time we found our own strength – the love within for our fellow man.

This look at the status quo is not criticism. It is just a fact. Anything that is independent of one's opinions, preferences, choices, advantages, and dogma, must be very strong, very clear. It must emerge out of certainty that is not shallow or biased.

Fact gives one courage, conviction, a daring quality that is never in revolt or reaction against the external. It has love to extend. And the peace you find becomes the peace of all humanity.

Do not deny it; do not accept it. You have the responsibility to see for yourself if it is a fact. There is the idea which is fictitious, and there is the fact. The wise deals with the fact and not the idea because ideas are abstract. Evasion into something abstract is never new. The new deals with the issue here and now. When you have stopped evading, then I would say that is something new.

To recognize the fact requires having the ears to hear. We must be responsible, for the external is only an extension of our own confusion and laziness. And things are getting worse and worse.

We may not be able to do anything about the government but we can be aware of what is not ethical. And then build our own life. I call that "New Age" – whereby we take responsibility for our own lives, for our own ethics, for our own virtue.

How are we to step out of a society in which we are bound by insecurity, bound to a job and to routine? We need indulgences just to cope with ourselves. There are more divorces, more crimes, more narcotics. There is more hate in the world, and greater tension and fear. If we value fear and insecurity, we will also value war.

The system is so strong that man is practically required to resort to wrong means in order to cope with it. Right means will have a tough time. There is obstacle after obstacle.

A person who is earnest and serious is already disillusioned. There is eagerness for correction; he does not pretend to know or not know. He questions and wants to know directly, not through the influence of another. And he must question because the vitality is in the question itself. Through questioning, we can free ourselves from opinions, assumptions, beliefs, conclusions, and consequences.

Negative thought is the highest form of thinking because it negates what is false. It undoes what is unreal. Positive thinking, on the other hand, asserts its authority and tends to make one fanatic. You cannot put truth in an idea or in a concept. Truth is free. And it is free when it has seen things that are unreal as unreal.

When we are free, then I would say there is something new. The new is within us, for the peace of God is within man. That is why all religions have emphasized, "KNOW THYSELF." [2] People who have that purity are the ones with no unfulfillment. They have found something within themselves. Doing takes second place to Being.

Being transcends personality and introduces us to something unlimited. Anything, then, that deals with what is God-created has that boundlessness about it. It is like Mother Teresa saying, "It is not a belief but a necessity"; she has something that is necessary. Mother Teresa exists independent of any ideas of a New Age. She is not of time.

I am talking about what makes an ordinary man a king – where nothing external or of consequences frightens him. He gives expression to what is new in himself. This is what we have to discover. The heart of a king trembles before a man who wants nothing.

It is self-discovery, not efficiency, that leads to the new action. This action is founded on the need to express the truth and love within you, rather than ambition and motive. This is where transformation takes place, and nothing can defeat it.

We must relate with the vibration of this land: "In God We Trust" and "All Men Are Created Equal." This is what America stands for. It is a new world. It must prepare itself to come to new consciousness.

Each person has a responsibility to love another – to look upon his fellow man only as God created him – because he has discovered there is no difference between himself and his brother.

This responsibility is yours.
To accept that responsibility
will transform your life.

CHAPTER ELEVEN

---

*The Kingdom is perfectly united
and perfectly protected,
and the ego will not prevail against it.
Amen.* [1]

11

DARK FORCES

AS WE LOOK at life upon this planet, we see there is great beauty in the movement of it, in the continuity of it. There is some other wisdom, some other intelligence behind it that sustains us with food, air, water, night, and day. It provides both our eyes and the light. It is not we who created the eyelids, nor even the miracle of the knee. There is no end of wonder about things. We are inspired to discover that there is some other force, some other intelligence of which we are a part.

Yet in the midst of the beauty of the manifested world, we have all but forgotten our Source and we live in a world of darkness.

You think you are the home of evil, darkness and sin. You think if anyone could see the truth about you he would be repelled, recoiling from you as if from a poisonous snake. You think if what is true about you were revealed to you, you would be struck with horror so intense that you would rush to death by your own hand, living on after seeing this being impossible.

...Today we question this, not from the point of view of what you think, but from a very different reference point, from which such idle thoughts are meaningless. These thoughts are not according to God's Will. These weird beliefs He does not share with you. This is enough to prove that they are wrong, but you do not perceive that this is so. [2]*

What are the dark forces that keep hidden from us the light and holiness that we are?

Dark forces can only be of one's own consciousness, some hidden fears in the recesses of the mind. Having forgotten the Name of God we have gotten caught in our jealousies and pettiness; in the uncleanliness of worry and selfishness; in the insecurity and non-forgiveness of attack thoughts; in the authority of problems that rule our lives. We have a cloud of dark forces that we project around us. We no longer have the confidence that we can call upon the memory of God that is within us.

See what has happened to mankind. For the most part we are panic-stricken, worn out; we lack the strength of character that could, for a split second, make a breakthrough in the bondage of time that we

---

* All quotations used in this chapter are from *A Course in Miracles.*

are in. We are dissipated and exhausted because there is so little virtue in our lives. What else could we do but project dark forces and be ruled by them?

When we are tense we want distractions, and we deny the opportunity to give expression to who we really are. We are forever giving expression to what we want to get away from. We are always running away – from ourselves. We use our inventions to run away from who we are. Stimulating experience is what we call progress: faster, louder, more destructive, always getting away. Are not dark forces at work within us?

Get to know yourself. Get to know how much loneliness rules you. Where there is loneliness, it has a partner named "fear." The two together have almost total control over us.

Fatigue and tension, too, are of dark forces, as are pressures and anxiety. We are no longer part of the rhythm of life, caught as we are in the grip of insecurity and worry. Anger, too, is planted in the brain of the man who is separated. It has deep roots. How would you uproot anger?

And in the midst of it we cannot recall the reality of who we really are. What could be worse?

We must wake up and see what we have done to our lives. Have we not become part of insanity and its destructiveness? Are not the dark forces stronger in our lives? Is there anything darker than the fear that constitutes insecurity?

And what do you think newspapers carry? Are they not the perpetuators of fear and violence and thus, promoters of dark forces? Do not be frightened of what dark forces are going to do. Just look at what they have already done and what they are doing now.

Each one of us is wrapped in our own survival. We are part of a very conditioned, centuries old, worn out brain, steeped in superstition and fear. Our thoughts emerge from this brain. What prevents us from being awakened from dark forces? The attractions and indulgence that make our lives so anxious and self-centered? Have we taken any interest in emptying ourselves of insecurity and problems, fear and unfulfillment? Why do we choose to live in the darkness of consequences? We are here to serve God, not expedience.

The situation demands that we come to a new strength, awakening different dimensions within ourselves and finding our greater potentials. If we are dependent on sensation we will never rise beyond it. Sensation is also part of dark forces. Try to step out of it and you will discover what hold it has. For us to survive upon the planet some of us must rise above sensation. Otherwise desire may well lead to the destruction of the world.

Only a few generations ago we had an ox for our plough, a horse for our carriage. Today it is the human being that is yoked to corporations. Dark forces are at work.

What we need to rise above sensation, the universities cannot impart. They merely provide skills for jobs – we are like beasts of burden. And so we have our jobs, our routines, our favorite outlets – the diversions and the distractions. It is called decadence, for it is self-destructive. There is no peace in it.

How rapidly we are losing the discrimination to see what is essential work and what is a mere job. Meaningful work is essential to a balanced life. Who but the few dare to overcome deeply ingrained insecurity, having found their own productive and meaningful work? Without fully understanding the work that balances life, idealism and realism cannot be reconciled.

Work is another name for realization, which means right livelihood, freedom from want, right-mindedness, and value. Realization frees us from external influences and makes us stand on our own, unafraid in the midst of a mercenary society.

To be self-reliant is the first step. Self-reliance is both a strength and a necessity. We think we under-stand it. Yet our intentions are but forms of wanting which we consider real. Thus, deception – an understanding that is not valid – continues its loveless existence and generates our present predicament.

Today, for the most part, we are more dull and more mediocre than ever before. That is the trend of decadence. It only leads us to more violence, more sensation, and more distractions in order to cope with our loneliness and boredom.

And where does all our energy go? Into self-destruction – on a national as well as individual level. Each person becomes an enemy to himself. That is certainly not the right use of God-given energy.

We have to wake up from this madness and insanity. It should concern each one of us that society is degenerating. You are an individual, a human being, created in the image of God. Will you not wake up from your slumber and indifference and recognize the holiness of your own life?

Our relationship with God is important, for it is real. And only those few who keep it intact leave upon the planet a voice that still vibrates and is alive. Without this, our relationships with one another – where jobs, money, and survival predominate – remain incomplete.

Discrimination is essential to know the false as the false. That which sees the false as the false is not the false. This seeing is the light that surrounds you and is ever with you.

We can begin by questioning everything. We can question the authority of dark forces, the authority of what conditions us. It is important that we see fatigue, anxiety, insecurity, and unfulfillment for what they are.

No matter how long the journey is, it does not begin until we take the first step.

Our function is to dissolve the dark forces and bring light where there is darkness.

It is your forgiveness that will bring the world of darkness to the light. It is your forgiveness that lets you recognize the light in which you see. Forgiveness is the demonstration that you are the light of the world. [3]

I am the light of the world [4] is real in us when we introduce forgiveness into our brain. Then there is no impurity, no animosity within the brain.

The purpose of the world you see is to obscure your function of forgiveness, and provide you with a justification for forgetting it. It is the temptation to abandon God and His Son by taking on a physical appearance. It is this the body's eyes look upon. [5]

Your picture of the world can only mirror what is within. The source of neither light nor darkness can be found without. Grievances darken your mind, and you look out on a darkened world. Forgiveness lifts the darkness, reasserts your will, and lets you look upon a world of light. [6]

When we have come to forgiveness, heaven's light will be ours, given to us and through us to all of mankind. Forgiveness dispels all fear, tension, and anxiety, for its light cannot be contaminated.

Let us be the light of the world that we are, for God Himself is in our mind.

Who is the light of the world except God's Son? This, then, is merely a statement of the truth about yourself. It is the opposite of a statement of pride, of arrogance, or of self-deception. It does not describe the self concept you have made. It does not refer to any of the characteristics with which you have endowed your idols. It refers to you as you were created by God. It simply states the truth.

...It is not humility to insist you cannot be the light of the world if that is the function God assigned to you.... This is a beginning step in accepting your real function on earth. [7]

To be the light of the world, then, is our function. It requires that we come to a deliberate decision to accept the attributes of God that we are. A deliberate decision is the action of the will. It brings a total renewal in one's whole being.

Either we trust in God, in the function He has given us, or we remain preoccupied with our own. This is the only decision. God's creation exists to bring man to his own holiness. God sees only perfection. This perfection, this light, has surrounded us from the beginning of time, even though we have been unaware of it.

When we are touched by the light of eternity, it introduces us to the love that is in our hearts. It is unlimited in its unfolding. One Buddha...and his light remains forever. It is always the One.

"I will there be light."

Today we are considering the will you share with God. This is not the same as the ego's idle wishes, out of which darkness and no-thingness arise. The will you share with God has all the power of creation in it.

...the light that shines upon this world reflects your will, and so it must be in you that we will look for it. [8]

This is where we will find it, within ourselves. Therefore, we are most blessed.

True light is strength, and strength is sinless-ness. If you remain as God created you, you must be strong and light must be in you. He Who ensured your sinlessness must be the guarantee of strength and light as well. You are as God created you. Darkness cannot obscure the glory of God's Son. You stand in light, strong in the sinlessness in which you were created, and in which you will remain throughout eternity. [9]

Our determination and the strength given to us for our integrity and resolve would overcome the issues we impose and project and perceive.

It is God's strength in you that is the light in which you see.... His strength denies your weakness. It is your weakness that sees through the body's eyes, peering about in darkness to behold the likeness of itself....

In darkness you perceive a self that is not there. Strength is the truth about you; weakness is an idol falsely worshipped and adored that strength may be dispelled, and darkness rule where God appointed that there should be light. [10]

We are more than personality. We are more than a body. We are of the spirit, created by God. The memory of God is inherent in each of us. Nothing can take it away.

The light of strength is constant, sure as love, forever glad to give itself away, because it cannot give but to itself. No one can ask in vain to share its sight, and none who enters its abode can leave without a miracle before his eyes, and strength and light abiding in his heart. [11]

No matter what the external circumstances are, it is always possible to come to our own light and the radiance of our own holiness. This light is the light that does not see through physical eyes. It is the light of eternity, the light of all creation.

This light sees what is of God, and it is holy. It is a light untouched by time, not limited to space. And a few moments of it are worth all of one's life, for we are then the Son of God extending the light of Heaven.

We must have faith that we are a child of God, the extension of His Love. Our yearning to recognize this as truth would bring us to that clarity, to that light. We must not allow anything to interfere with that. And if we get distracted we need not blame ourselves. We just need to start over again.

> Your sinlessness is guaranteed by God. Over and over this must be repeated, until it is accepted. It is true. Your sinlessness is guaranteed by God. Nothing can touch it, or change what God created as eternal. The self you made, evil and full of sin, is meaningless. Your sinlessness is guaranteed by God, and light and joy and peace abide in you. [12]

Let us not hold negative thoughts about ourselves or another, for they are like dark clouds within us. By this means, we overcome the world.

The whole earth becomes a host to the child of God and pays homage to his presence that brings peace. All of nature longs, yearns, and waits for such a person. That person is you.

> O my brothers, if you only knew the peace that will envelop you and hold you safe and pure and lovely in the Mind of God, you could but rush to meet Him where His altar is. Hallowed your name and His, for they are joined here in this holy place. Here He leans down to lift you up to Him, out of illusions into holiness; out of the world and to eternity; out of all fear and given back to love. [13]

CHAPTER TWELVE

---

*There is a point
beyond which illusions cannot go.* [1]

12

THE FORCES
THAT SWAY HUMANITY

To ALL but a few people the gradual decline in man's relationship with God, in man's relationship with man, and in man's relationship with nature is obvious. The word "democracy" no longer has the same meaning it had when it first found its voice. Religion, too, was to mean something totally different than what it now represents to the mass of humanity. Religion is no longer the actuality of a state of being where duality ends, where one harnesses the energy of Truth itself and comes to clarity. The same unrelatedness is true of economy and technology.

Interpretation is a major factor in this deterioration. It has little to do with reality because it is based on opinion and assumption. And where these are prevalent, there always lurks vested interest. Thus, selfish motives, ambition, and fragmentation continue to thrive. Is there not always one group or segment of society that benefits at the expense of another?

In what way has education or religion, economy or technology, or even politics – the forces that sway humanity – contributed to bringing the human being to precision, self-honesty, or freedom? What political system supports the brotherhood of man or the humanizing of existence on earth? Is not the loss of self-honesty greater than the so-called gain in expedience? Shortsighted views have nothing to do with truth or the understanding of reality. Prosperity and affluence, devoid of conviction, must inevitably collapse.

The people who are "civilized" are usually not productive in the real sense of the word, for they do not bring that which is of Heaven to earth. Their vision is not holy. They do not work with divine energies. Only the one who is co-creator is truly productive and civilized. The fragmented being promotes disharmony. Self-convinced, he exploits man with his horizontal values and beliefs. And under a myriad of disguises, man is misled.

Of what use is commercialized affluence to a man of wisdom and simplicity? The individual has so much to outgrow. Yet what is genuine in the individual is created in the image of God, and it is always with him.

In this civilization most human energy is drained for unessentials. The captive employees of corporations are cast aside in their old age without having come to their own self-sufficiency. They die hardly knowing anything of relationship.

Relationship is the miracle of oneness.

The agony of separation, with its preoccupation with survival and constant need of gratification, is all most of us have known. Most people die knowing neither wholeness nor the peace that surpasses understanding. [2] There is hardly a face that is itself, or a voice that is direct or uncontaminated.

The industrial economy has assumed dominant importance and "jobs" have become as significant as Life itself. Without a career one cannot survive in the system. From childhood we are trained to make a living, and insecurity has become the premise of modern existence. We are left with trained skills, not the certainty of direct knowing.

It is difficult for self-honesty to survive in present conditions. We are reduced to being a consumer. And with the advent of electronics that surpass human capabilities, unemployment is the inevitable challenge before mankind. This challenge, which is born out of a lack of ethics, cannot be resolved without virtue in the individual life.

A life of routine and compromises, inconsistent with our inner calling, must result in violence and disharmony. Internally we are poor in proportion to the externalized prosperity we seek. So much of wisdom and simplicity is lost. Human warmth and the hospitality of family life are all but gone.

What is man without divine leisure – the space a human being needs to know his own wholeness, the potentials of all levels of his being?

Society is caught in thought forms, belief systems, and bureaucracy. It cannot assimilate newness; and growth, if any, becomes external and horizontal and fails to elevate the spirit of man. This is the twelfth hour. Everywhere there is disillusionment and questioning. Faith in the Presidency is declining. Peace treaties and political alliances have little meaning beyond temporary convenience. Where are ethics and morality in a world that gives importance to pleasure, gratification, and power? Walk the streets and see the banks, insurance companies, and the cult of restlessness – not temples of the spirit, not shrines reflecting the vertical relationship of man with God.

Education and technology are seldom directed towards inner awakening or inner purity, nor towards the removal of deception. Even so-called reform in such a society is but reaction and change at the same level; hence, no change at all. It is merely a shift of emphasis, or more military sophistication and hardware, or a better way of computerizing the profiteering mind. It gives rise to more and more nationalism and conformity.

Outlets flourish to relieve the stress where life has become but a routine function. Confronted with a challenge, those with very little inner strength quickly fall back on habit patterns. One way or another the status quo continues in its helplessness, and the transformation of man becomes increasingly difficult.

In the absence of humanism, the compelling circumstances ahead of America will have their impact. Technology may well begin to fail. Education without morality will be ineffective. The economy is likely to decline.

The masses may even revert to the calling of "religion." It is irresistible in its appeal, especially under the present pressures. The call of "back to God and back to prayer," with all its tyranny of fanaticism, may duplicate in America the religious cry of Islam in the Middle East.

True religion, however, is not a dogma or a set of beliefs; it is a state of being that ends duality and alternatives. In it there can be no hate or revenge, no punishment or cruelty. Real religion is the state of Love. It excludes no one.

As long as unfulfillment and insecurity are not dealt with, however, we are compelled to externalize our life. Ambition, fear, and selfishness become inevitable, making us inconsiderate of another, and in the end, ourselves. Thus, we become self-destructive.

Even eating has become a perversion. The food we consume is increasingly artificial. The clothes we wear are mostly synthetic. Even the insensitivity of bleached hair is appalling. It is a preference for death rather than life.

Throughout history mankind has had faith in government, in prosperity, in religion, in education; these became the driving forces that swayed humanity. Man has changed from illiteracy to education, from poverty to prosperity, from primitive labor to sophisticated technology. But somehow we have come to an end in spite of the progress we have made. We have arrived at disillusionment. What we thought would solve our problems has not done so. The solution is not external.

Society will not change, but the individual can still rise to the height of his own being and relate with the reality within.

We have listened to goals and ideals that stimulated our self-interest: prosperity, equality, freedom, all the grandiose phraseology. How few, however, have evolved to find their own perfection in the living moment. Very few human beings have seen through their projected deceptions and saved themselves from the commotion of wasted lives.

Now one wonders if there is any learning through experience at all. Mr. J. Krishnamurti said, "Freedom is at the beginning, not at the end." [3] Wisdom avoids going through the experience of trial and error; it is awakened by the clarity within that sets one free from illusions and deceptions.

We have to heed the voice of vertical men such as Lao Tzu, Jefferson, Thoreau, and Gandhi, for they are not echoes of borrowed thoughts. How little have we heeded their clear voices, or the small voice within ourselves that leads us to the wisdom of simplicity.

We seek to solve problems and are taught to do so without realizing that there are no problems apart from the mind. What are problems? They are always related to fear and self-centeredness. And what is self but an abstraction manufactured by thought? Where is the clarity that dissolves all problems and the duality of thought itself?

To die to the self is the big fear. We have to have the courage of honesty and integrity to overcome fear, and then to die to all the conditioning and the illusions of the world. Then we will see there are no such things as problems.

Who has learned to end inner turmoil? The conflicting forces that sway humanity are all we know as long as we are subject to circumstances and consequences.

We have yet to learn to "TURN THE CHEEK." [4] What impact upon humanity such an action would have. What purity, this Christ-like action!

What, then, will end the sway of conflicting forces on humanity?

A point of non-deviation: the ending of separation from God. As long as there are alternatives to this, the shift and sway are inevitable and life remains personal, tribal in its approach, caught in choices and preferences, and caught in fragmentation.

When alternatives end we inherit the energy of Truth – the truth of Love. It is the Given made accessible to the receptive mind. And it is given to you to give.

CHAPTER THIRTEEN

*The certain are perfectly calm,
because they are not in doubt.*

*They do not raise questions,
because nothing questionable enters their minds.
This holds them in perfect serenity,
because this is what they share,
knowing what they are.* [1]

13

THE STILL MIND
IS NOT SWAYED

Perhaps the best way to begin
is to present a fact. A fact exists in the Present. It is
not abstract. The fact I would like to explore comes
from the question: what is a "mandala"?

The first part of the word, "man," means, in
Punjabi, the mind – the Mind of God. "Dala" is what
you put into it. Because our mind becomes what we
put into it, we are conscious only of the content of our
mind. Thus, what we put into our mind is our
responsibility. This is a fact. If we put anxiety,
problems, and assumptions into our mind, then we
become these. By so doing we have deviated and
separated from the all-pervasive Mind of God. The
duality in our experience appears because of this
separation.

The Mind of God is a state of being – creative and energetic. It is a fact. In the state of the Mind of God, there is truth. Truth is never endangered.

Our mind – not to be confused with the physical brain – is part of the Mind of God. If we put fear into it, then we become fear and we extend fear. Fear is an idea, and like all ideas, abstract. We have mistaken the brain to be the Mind although it is only a storehouse of memory. It would require being alive to the clarity of the present moment to undo the bondage of our own little knowings, so easily threatened.

A Course in Miracles states,

> *Nothing real can be threatened.*
> *Nothing unreal exists.* [2]

Opinions are endangered. Assumptions are endangered. These are the things we put into the mandala, the wholeness of mind. Therefore, we must be careful not to put into it what is not of God, for if we do we isolate ourselves in our continual preoccupation with our personal dilemma. We must keep this mandala uncontaminated or we will not know we are an extension of God and that our minds are joined. We face a tremendous responsibility.

When personalized activity begins, the search begins, the struggle begins, the improvement courses begin, and we move further away from stillness, from our reality. There are no means to get there, for we are It.

We are so frightened of stillness. We think we need activity. And then we divide it into good or bad, right or wrong. We never seem to see the duality and conflict we initiate.

As we go beyond the right and wrong there is a space of clarity and truth where love is the only surety. It is beyond words. This stillness of the mind that is whole, so energetic in its intensity, is creative and productive in the real sense. The man who is whole is co-creator with God Himself.

The energy of stillness is the only thing in creation that is productive, for it is not personal. It affects the very atmosphere of the planet. Personal activity brings about war, hate, and fear. A still mind, at peace, is a benediction. It is a state in which we are not dependent on anything, not even learning.

The preoccupation of "learning" is a nuisance we must end. We have always been fascinated by it and self-convinced that we wanted to know and live by truth. But we used the preoccupation itself to actually evade what we were seeking. In this there is an inherent deception.

In the Mind of God, all search, all self-improvement, all learning ends in the discovery of the perfection that we are. From then on, whatever we do is an extension of that perfection. What we are is far superior to what we want to become.

We are caught in the idea of becoming. The personal mind – which in reality is the brain with its physical senses – becomes any idea it formulates. But awareness is never contaminated. The awakened mind never deviates into abstract thought. It dissolves it.

Ideas are dissolved in attention and we remain the Mind of God upon which nothing intrudes. Otherwise, we are in the bondage of ideas which make life at once abstract and personal; and we remain separated from the Reality that we are.

Awareness leads one to God's perspective. Thought never does. Thought is always a point of view. Awareness and its observation have the potential to dissolve ideas. We assumed that to dissolve the idea and come to clarity required effort.

To dissolve all ideas and come to a wholeness, whereby nothing is outside of us, is to affect the very planet and the destiny of the stars. Wholeness has the purity of innocence and the space of the universe.

It is innocence that experiences the glory, the perfection, and the holiness of the Mind of God that we are. Nothing is outside of it – not even God.

Innocence is an attribute of humility, the most powerful thing in creation; it is untouched by fear. To that state every thought is external. Even the body is external. That state is religious.

Religion is a state of being, not a system of beliefs or dogma. It is not fragmented into Christianity or Buddhism, Hinduism or Islam. It suffers no division and encompasses all people. True religion is not a means of self-improvement. It sees that we are already perfect, as God made us.

There are many deceptions that we do not question. How many of us realize that nationalism is poisonous and produces war, and that only in the man-made world do we live and die?

Experience, time, and selfhood being our only reference points, we build a personal world of survival and success. Disappointment reoccurs repeatedly but no disillusion – the awakening within oneself. There is hardly anyone who encourages our rebirth out of cause and effect, the knowing that is not knowing at all. Yet we believe in our personal world without question; never knowing peace, we know only a life of reaction.

Can we begin to see the wrong premises upon which human society's belief system is based? Not much is done to encourage us to outgrow it, but much is done to encourage our pursuit of self-improvement so that we remain within the system.

In my younger days I was tempted to wallow in the ordeal of self-improvement and pursue my own projections of sitting in the Himalayas cross-legged – all the self-torture and penance that goes on with religious life. The tendency for activity is so strong in us. Curiosity assumes the importance of learning and gives us juicy preoccupations. We feel very holy punishing and denying ourselves. To come to clarity is to question these very thoughts, however.

The word religion also means "dialogue" – where two or more meet in His Name. Dialogue demands an intensity of interest that is not caught in concepts and does not promote one's own opinion. Thus, religion, too, is not a mere exchange of ideas or mutual agreement; its energy ends the separation between the two, the duality.

But throughout the ages, what has man reduced religion to! Behold the treatment of those whose lives expressed eternity: Christ is crucified, Joan of Arc is burned, Socrates poisoned.

Accused of corrupting the youth of Athens, Socrates said at his trial that the lawyers had not spoken a word of truth and yet they even had him convinced. This is how clever expressions can be where fear and disquietude rule. Socrates, the man of eternal voice, was sentenced to death.

According to Plato's account, a friend of Socrates later bribed his guards and made arrangements for his escape. He went to Socrates, urging him to make haste.

What do you think Socrates would say? The man of God who never deviates from the Mind of God, how would he respond? Would he personalize his situation and stray from the action of Life, or say something new that no man has ever said before, something original born out of the intensity of the Present?

The still mind is ever creative and productive. It is not subject to time. It has no preference in circumstances. It hears the Voice of the Universe.

Socrates said to the friend,

"It is never right to do a wrong or return a wrong or defend one's self against injury by retaliation...." [3]

How beautiful! To know truth would require stillness. Stillness conquers fear and remains unaffected by anything external. It is an internal action within oneself which ends duality and brings consistency to all levels of one's being.

The still mind is undeceived. It is a state of fulfillment without which there is no integrity in life. Once you have that fulfillment, you can no longer be part of man-made religions or politics. You are out of it all. And your being affects everything that is. You love everyone because all are part of the Mind of God. Others may be doing things out of hate, but your love for the human being is not affected.

The planet needs our love. It needs the peace that we extend. Our reverence for plants, flowers, and animals is essential. We need to understand the stillness and glory of twilight that brings holiness into being. We need to understand the awakening energy of the dawn. Man is necessary on this planet in order to bring the Kingdom of God to earth. The planet is deprived of heavenly vibrations without him.

We are all part of the same life. There is no separation between "you" and "me." There is only the one Will of God we all share. Reality is what God extends; therefore, you and I are actually what God is – an extension of that state, that peace. This may well be the only thing we need to learn. But educated ignorance has not helped us to do so, any more than the natural ignorance we had when we were illiterate.

Today, you rarely meet anyone who lives outside of conditioned social patterns. There is no one so totally free of them, liberated with a radiance of his own, like Jesus saying,

"LET THE DEAD BURY THEIR DEAD." [4]

Ours has been a tribal approach to a vast issue of life, with its resulting fragmentation. We are part of that tribal approach the minute we deviate from stillness, no matter who we are or what we are doing.

When I came to the United States I sensed a tremendous vitality. The unique vibrations of America began by integrating people of all nations and religions. As integration takes place, we move towards wholeness – allowing other people to be what they are, not relating with any belief system but with the fact that we are all part of the same life we all share. It is no longer a concept called brotherhood. It is the actuality of brotherhood, lived.

The still mind no longer has boundaries and no longer thinks that you are an enemy because you hold different belief systems. Beliefs separate us; the still mind encompasses all people. The still mind holds the world in its palm, caresses it, and blesses it.

Find your own stillness and you will discover the forces of that inwardness, of that wholeness, of that which is the Unknown. Lift the veil, and It is.

CHAPTER FOURTEEN

14

COMING EVENTS
CAST THEIR SHADOW

WHENEVER a nation stands aloof from virtue and ethics, it becomes beguiled by the world of the senses. To the extent materialism succeeds, man becomes inwardly weak; and this is happening all over the world today. A preoccupation with buying, selling, loss, and gain prevails in the absence of love and goodness. It is a fraud against humanity. What influence will today's controlled multitude have on the new generation? Wisdom is required to turn the tide.

Humanism demands a change. That is the New World's destiny: to awaken itself and revolutionize the world. Humanism then flowers into self-reliance, having something of one's own to give, and finally, into service. But in this age of dependence on jobs how can one know and honor humanism? How can an accelerated society heed the call to wisdom of its forefathers, "In God We Trust"?

Because America was the undisputed leader after World War II, whatever example it set would determine the trend for the rest of the planet. If the United States had cooperated with goodness and rightness, she could have lifted up the whole planet. This opportunity never existed before.

America could have caused a change. If she had she would have recognized and cooperated with leaders who had different values and ethics – the noble and wise – in other parts of the world. The premise of our foreign policy would have been very different. We could have produced a world free of war, rather than one of political power blocs.

America's industrial affluence was an experiment for the world. Why did it not set a new, humanistic course, but compel the world to militarize?

Gradually, a small minority began to monopolize political, military and industrial interests. They exaggerated the fear of communism and invented the Cold War. But perhaps most damaging, this small anti-democratic group which perpetrated a fraud upon the American people also became the enemies of wisdom throughout the world. Consistently, the wise, objective voices of other nations were ignored. Even today the independent voices of America itself are not fully heeded. There are consequences when a nation does not listen to those who have outgrown nationalism and society.

Today the planet has become divided in the interests of manmade dogmas seeking control over the minds of men, women, and children. A concentration of power in the hands of the few not only misleads but imposes a limitation upon its people.

When America wanted military bases in Egypt, ostensibly to counter the Soviet Union, Egyptian President Nasser said that his country feared "these defense pacts are a new sort of colonialism." He noted that Britain and France had dominated the Middle East for a long time while Russia had never had any influence there.

President Nasser added that at the end of World War II, "the Middle East was looking to America as the saviour, the new country that was rising to liberate us from domination. We were looking to America with faith." But within a decade Nasser was disillusioned, seeing that "you [America] supported the colonial countries against the countries who want to be free."

One wonders what the facts actually were, and who decided that Russia was a threat in the Middle East? The media usually prints what government officials say, and soon most people are thinking similarly. Even Thomas Jefferson said, however,

> "The man who never looks into a newspaper is better informed than he who reads them, inasmuch as he who knows nothing is nearer the truth than he whose mind is filled with falsehoods and errors."

Strong nations seek to exact global influence either through colonial occupation, the establishment of military bases, or various forms of economic and political intervention. It is this involvement in the affairs of others, as well as the exercise of force needed to maintain this position, which produces consequences. After the second World War America could have turned the tide to value humanism and goodness over its own military, economic, or political interests. But this challenge demanded wisdom.

America often violated its democratic principles and got involved in the affairs of other countries. Howard Zinn, in his book, *A People's History of the United States*, writes:

> "By the end of the Vietnam War, 7 million tons of bombs had been dropped on Vietnam, more than twice the total bombs dropped in Europe and Asia in World War II – almost one 500-pound bomb for every human being in Vietnam. In addition, poisonous sprays were dropped by planes to destroy trees and any kind of growth – an area the size of the state of Massachusetts was covered with such poison."

Millions of Vietnamese lost their lives, 58,000 Americans were killed and 365,000 Americans were wounded in the war. The money spent totalled over $172 billion. How great was the cost of the Vietnam War in terms of human life? How great was the profit made by the military-industrial complex? It was an utterly unessential war, but surely profitable to the arms manufacturers and other industries.

And yet there were wise voices who offered warning, including Indian Prime Minister Indira

Gandhi. Buckminster Fuller, speaking of her in an inscription, wrote:

> "To Indira, in whose integrity God is entrust-
> ing much of the evolutionary success of
> humanity and with utter safety." [1]

Shortly before her assassination at the hands of her bodyguards, she herself wrote:

> "If I die a violent death as some fear and a
> few are plotting, I know the violence will be
> in the thought and the action of the
> assassin, not in my dying...." [2]

She warned the U.S. regarding the escalation of war in Indochina, urging us that war should be against poverty not against communism.

French President Charles de Gaulle had with-drawn from Vietnam to focus on his own country's needs. In June, 1961, at a meeting in Paris with President John Kennedy, he said:

> "You will find that intervention in this area
> will be an endless entanglement. Once a
> nation has been aroused, no foreign power,
> however strong, can impose its will upon it.
> You will discover this for yourselves. For
> even if you find local leaders who in their
> own interests are prepared to obey you, the
> people will not agree to it, and indeed do not
> want you. The ideology you invoke will make
> no difference. Indeed, in the eyes of the
> masses it will become identified with your

will to power. That is why the more you become involved out there against Communism, the more the Communists will appear as the champions of national independence, and the more support they will receive, if only from despair....I predict that you will sink step by step into a bottomless military and political quagmire, however much you spend in men and money. What you, we and others ought to do for unhappy Asia is not to take over the running of these States ourselves, but to provide them with the means to escape from the misery and humiliation which, there as elsewhere, are the causes of totalitarian regimes. I tell you this in the name of the West." [3]

Former Indian Prime Minister Jawaharlal Nehru was a statesman whom President John Kennedy had compared to Abraham Lincoln. One need only read his account, *Glimpses Of World History*, to make contact with his enormous scope of mind. His was a voice of sanity in an unstable world. Former United Nations Secretary General U Thant said of Jawaharlal Nehru:

"He was not only a great man, but a good man. His extraordinary qualities endeared him not only to the people of India but to people all over the world who had at heart peace, justice and equality for mankind." [4]

French President Charles de Gaulle said of Pandit Nehru:

"This great man, for whom the cause of humanity was inseparable from the cause of the Indian people, his plans continually disappointed by the magnitude of the task, but unshakable in his faith and unwearying in his efforts, outlined to me the gigantic problems of subsistence and unity with which his country was faced, and the ways in which mine might help to alleviate them, not without ultimate benefit to herself." [5]

Prime Minister Nehru, in a United Nations speech, spoke about:

"...a world without war – a world based on the cooperation of nations and peoples. It is not merely a world where war is kept in check, or a balancing of armed forces. It is much deeper than that. It is a world from which the major causes of war have been removed, and social structures built up which further peaceful cooperation, within a nation, as well as between nations."

America presently enjoys an external security built on fear. Yet we must realize that true security lies in rightness. Can America afford peace now? Will industrialization allow it? There are times when one wonders who owns the government.

On June 7, 1981, then Speaker of the House of Representatives, Mr. Thomas (Tip) O'Neill, appeared on ABC's *Issues and Answers*. He said that America's political system was being controlled by the "selfish" – the wealthy, upper echelon of the nation. He warned that the middle American who built the country upon certain principles and ideals was being forgotten and could one day wake up to find that America had been destroyed.

A wise head of state does not resort to expedience and compromise. Having reverence for Life, he has recognized the inflexible law of cause and effect which regulates external forces and has dire consequences.

One who will not contradict the Will of God discovers that non-cooperation and economic sanctions will work to resolve international disputes and lead mankind to a war-free world. When kindness and friendship with another nation fails to end disagreement, the wisdom of non-violence and non-cooperation will succeed if moral strength accompanies them.

On August 2, 1990, Iraqi soldiers invaded Kuwait. The United Nations called for the imposition of economic sanctions on Iraq. The exclusive use of sanctions could have ushered in an age in which war was abolished. On January 17, 1991, however, a military force dominated by America launched a full-scale bombing campaign against Iraq. Of the 2,000 combat aircraft flown, approximately 1,800 were American.

The loss of sanctions as a means of peaceful resolution is a tragedy. It may have required years for the goals of the sanctions to be accomplished, but they could have been made to work for humanity's sake if the intent was one of peace. To end war is a just and noble aspiration in man. The harmony between America and the Soviet Union offered the opportunity to direct money and skills toward honoring the sacredness of life on the planet.

Instead, the resulting war with Iraq publicized American industry's modern weapons, and at the same time displayed the ineffectiveness of other nation's military hardware, now rendered virtually obsolete.

America's preparation for war in the Persian Gulf had actually begun years before. According to government figures, from 1982 through 1989 the U.S. alone sold $24.5 billion worth of military equipment to Saudi Arabia.

An essay by Strobe Talbott in the January 13, 1992, *Time Magazine* reported:

> "In November 1990, during the buildup to Operation Desert Storm, James Baker tried to shore up support on the home front for the dispatch of U.S. troops half a world away. 'To bring it down to the level of the average American citizen,' he said, 'standing up to Saddam Hussein *means jobs*.' Then, to make sure everyone understood, he did it again, 'If you want to sum it up in one word, it's *jobs*.'"

Is it true that America has come to the point where wars have become a political and commercial necessity? Only kindness and compassion can succeed in humanizing society. The question is, "Can America afford a world free of war?"

"Might is right" may appeal to the profiteering segment of society, but it inevitably results in disaster – first abroad and then at home. The awesome national debt will compel the government to resort to unthinkable justifications. Irresponsibility and our perfected military machine could lead prosperous America to lean and hungry days at home.

Sadly, even before reaching maturity the United States began to decline. Within a decade America has become the largest debtor nation in the world. Its immense national debt will be a liability for generations to come. The cost of paying interest on the current debt of $3.7 trillion will be approximately $23.5 million per hour in 1992. [6]

The following is an excerpt from economist, diplomat, and author John Kenneth Galbraith's editorial on "The Price of Comfort" which appeared in newspapers across the country on January 6, 1991.

> "In the United States, the price of past error has reached truly formidable proportions and with, alas, consequences going far beyond our frontiers. There has been much discussion in these last years of the increasing interdependence of nations – the global economy. One consequence is that all must suffer for the actions and errors of any one government and people, and especially if they are those of a country as large and important on the world scene as the United States.

"The American prospect, as we enter the second year of the new decade and end 10 years of free-enterprise rediscovery in Washington, is far from bright. And from the United States the shadow of financial instability, economic recession, unemployment and uncertain government extends out to the world."

Despite enormous debt and rising unemployment, the five days of presidential inaugural festivities in 1989 cost $30 million, making it the most expensive inauguration in America's history.

When a country is rich and in control, it is a law – like the lion in the jungle. But the little cubs also grow and eventually take the old lion's place. There may well be violence as America weakens. Not having given importance to moral strength within, America will continue to rely on the external. It may result in a police state, for nothing is going to be safe. People will be subjected to more and more conformity and control. The situation could be conducive to a military takeover. The externals are in control when man lacks moral values. It is as if people are drugged by outlets and pacified with indulgences.

Nothing the world has ever faced will resemble what will happen in America, since we have violated right relationship with the land, sea, and sky. Nature too may revolt. Deterioration is flourishing and the world is caught in the horrible grip of consequences.

As America declines, what will happen in the rest of the world? Two expansionary nations achieved prominence after World War II – Israel and China. Right now America supports them both. But the future belongs to China.

China has become strong because in its isolation – imposed by the West for decades – it had to come to self-sufficiency. Indian Prime Minister Indira Gandhi said,

> "Perhaps if China had not been so isolated it wouldn't have been so aggressive. It would have been more possible to bring it within a certain discipline." [7]

For years, as an act of intimidation, America paraded its Seventh Fleet up and down the waters of China's coast. America also acknowledged the tiny island of Formosa as the real China and effectively campaigned to keep mainland China out of the United Nations. That was the case until U.S. business interests determined that in order to obtain a new marketplace, mainland China would have to be recognized. Overnight the "red" in Red China disappeared without a trace.

Destiny and the West's consequences combine to pass leadership to another people. Today the Arabs are divided and lack leadership. But China will ally with the Asian nations and give them the strength they have longed for. Central Asia's Moslems – whose energies and capacities are more advanced than those of some of the desert dwellers – will join with China and the Arab world to challenge the declining West. The two factors – expansion and alliance – may very well make it possible for China to extend all the way to the Mediterranean. China has a destiny. All the yellow races are rising as though preordained.

Japan, too, through the efficiency of manufacturing is compelling the U.S. automobile industry to falter in its attempt to survive. Other industries will follow. America could never have imagined that her international dominance of the aerospace industry would be threatened by Japan but it is only a matter of time before Japan will surpass her in the manufacturing of commercial aircraft.

America's last chance was to ally with Russia. But we did not support the wise statesman, Mikhail Gorbachev, who oversaw the bloodless dismantling of an empire. One wonders whether capitalism could end without bloodshed. Russia walked out of country after country it had controlled, and divided up its own political union. Will America be as farsighted when Alaska and Hawaii want to be independent of the United States?

We did not recognize Mikhail Gorbachev's unique voice, nor appreciate his nobility. One is baffled that such wisdom was accessible to mankind. How few were aware of it. America now gives preferred trading status to China which massacred its dissident students in Tiananmen Square. In doing so America is cooperating with its future rival, and has opposed the Russians who need friendship and help. Hardly anyone pays much heed to the widespread inconsistencies. What causes this indifference?

Mikhail Gorbachev stayed consistent with his principles as he gave freedom to Eastern Europe.

People were allowed to choose their governments even though Gorbachev knew they might go against him. Most politicians would not have been able to give up that power without violence. As with other great beings throughout history, his seeming failure was his greatest success. Mikhail Gorbachev's loss of political power, and the subsequent ending of the Soviet Union, represents the world's inability to embrace his uncompromising wisdom.

Around this time Poland and other newly-democratic countries appealed to the U.S. for economic aid. But what they were given was not in proportion to their human needs. One cannot help but question how much more help Poland would have received if it had been in an armed struggle with communist Russia.

Military aid is the focal point of America's foreign policy. So much U.S. money has been poured into the Philippines and Pakistan that one would think they should be industrial giants by now. But the assistance is largely in the form of military hardware to these non-democratic nations. From 1954 to 1963, America spent over $1 billion supplying and training Pakistan's armed forces.

Who provided the funds, and who realizes the benefits? Do living standards for Filipinos and Pakistanis improve as a result of military assistance? Does trade with U.S. companies increase? Does goodwill rise between the nations? Recently Imelda Marcos, widow of the former ruler of the Philippines, was arrested in Manila. She was accused of stealing as much as $5 billion during the twenty-year Marcos dictatorship, much of which was paid by American taxpayers. Yet, she and her husband, Ferdinand Marcos, were welcomed and honored as guests of the American people. Where the "laws of justice have become subject to the laws of injustice,"[8] the consequences are that we have little that is vertical to impart to the next generation. How can we expect our children to listen to our words which are devoid of truth and thoughtfulness?

America's downfall began with abuse of human potential and the misuse of industrial might. Its industries sought profit in promoting a life of artificiality, not in meeting the primary needs of man on which survival rests.

What we are describing here may seem negative, but one needs to see what is ahead. America's lifestyle of outlets, indulgences, and distractions may well come to an end. The discovery of inner resources has not been a national priority. Instead, we have externalized our lives to a dangerous degree. There is inherent disorder in over-externalization and frustration.

Will economic chaos wake up the American people? Perhaps mass unemployment and the challenge to easy and comfortable lives will bring about a change of values.

To make internal correction is probably the least enticing path to take. We face, at every turn, external opposition from society's vested interests by which we are virtually controlled, as well as all our own fears and misperceptions. However, the will to exchange fear for love is always there. We need to make contact with our everlasting holiness and peace, gather our own strength, and not be affected by the externals.

Our pressured lives today hardly allow the entry of awareness. There is just the compelling urge to join the collective, to revel in "the highest standard of living in the world." Such pressure dampens the sanity of stillness and forbids a life of serenity. It rules us, and does not even give the space to question the momentum of a world where half-truths have become an expedience.

Only wisdom and humanism are free of conflict and consequences. Humanism has no outer activity. But we are drawn to activities, which then pressure us. And a pressured person likes affluence, because it provides outlets and indulgences. Pleasure's stimulation makes us dependent on pleasure itself, whereas serenity, having its own inner potentials, is ever free.

Emerson had said,

> "There are people who have an appetite for grief, pleasure is not strong enough...."

For decades, America has wallowed in the world of pleasure even while it was inflicting the pain of war upon weaker nations halfway around the world. The era of pleasure is coming to an end, and grief is staring us in the face. How will the mercenary civilization tied to jobs deal with it when there is not the strength of rightness in their lives?

whereas serenity, having its own inner potentials, is
ever free.

Emerson said,

> "There are people who have an appetite for
> grief, pleasure is not strong enough...."

For decades, America has wallowed in the world
of pleasure even while it was inflicting the pain of war
upon weaker nations halfway around the world. The
era of pleasure is coming to an end, and grief is staring
us in the face. How will the mercenary civilization tied
to jobs deal with it when there is not the strength of
rightness in their lives?

Mother Teresa said,

> "There are people in America that are so
> lonely they wish they could die."

There is an urgent need in America to take care of
those living in the slums, the tens of thousands of
people in the large cities that are compelled to live at
a sublevel of existence. According to the *Children's
Defense Fund* every 35 seconds an infant is born into
poverty in the United States and every 14 minutes an
American infant dies in the first year of life.

During the six weeks the U.S. was fighting in the
Persian Gulf, according to the *National Association of
Religious Women*, 1,250 U.S. infants and children died
from poverty, 4,000 died due to low birth weight, and
1,825 were killed or injured by guns. Is not the human
being more important than building a war machine or

spending hundreds of billions of dollars on space exploration?

The New World is a land of abundance in a world haunted by famine. Wars in the future could be fought over food supplies. Now life gives humanity a space in which to change. We have a decade to correct our outlook.

A change of presidents is not going to make much difference because the President represents and is part of mass consciousness. The political situation is such that most of the same Congressmen and Senators return to Washington after each election. Mere enthusiasm will not correct the approach to life that has become the genetic pattern of America. Any real correction can take place after the lean years; the true spirit of America will rise. Whoever undermines the Divine Emanation of man sees only blood and bones. The New World will come to its own expression for the first time.

In the end, neither materiality nor poverty is the issue. Man's separation from wholeness is the issue. Within wholeness everything extends what it is, and there is a sharing of love that intensifies the Source of Creation. Without the light of the heart our lives are meaningless; without the love of honesty it is not possible to make contact with the sacredness within. It is gratefulness that introduces man to humanism.

Humanism and the reversal process could begin in America. The underdeveloped Third World is too enamored by indulgent Western lifestyles to consider changing. But in America, disillusionment and transformation are possible. America is energetic. It need not go towards violence. America could become the first nation to realize that affluence without wisdom is self-destructive. It could totally change the vibration of the planet.

Now that America is the only superpower, non-violence is possible. War can be abolished and the New World's destiny of bringing peace and prosperity to all mankind can be fulfilled. America can restore credibility to the use of economic sanctions rather than destructive force in the resolution of international disputes. Through arms control, it could also prevent other ambitious nations from becoming superpowers.

America has to change its own relationship to the United Nations and allow the U.N. to honor its original intent, so that poorer nations are helped rather than manipulated in the interest of political power blocs. We have to rise to a non-nationalistic perspective.

The population explosion of the Third World has gotten out of control, and resources at the level of nationalism cannot deal with it. It is a problem that can be solved only at the human level, for the resources are there. Goodwill in America is enough to awaken mankind to a New Age by putting energy into solving the problems of over-population. Similarly, it can meet the primary needs of mankind everywhere.

In 1948, America initiated the Point Four Program, known as the Marshall Plan. It said, "The only war we seek is the war against poverty, disease, illiteracy, and hunger." Later, however, it became subject to political intrigue. It is now time for us to recognize that only humanism is consistent with meeting the primary needs of man for food, shelter, and clothing. This must be kept free from politics and preferences.

We have the technology to help all nations meet their needs and move towards self-sufficiency. It could become a joyous joint venture where profit is not the motive. In doing so America would benefit along with the rest of humanity. Shifting attention and production toward sanity would solve the problem of unemployment. Only by feeding the hungry of the world will we be able to feed our own people, subject as they are to jobs.

The goodness and right use of science, technology, and industry would enliven America and honor the spirit of "In God We Trust." In the end, "In God We Trust" could become a benediction to all mankind. Goodness cannot fail. The American people would respond to it. Turning to rightness demands conviction, but there is no risk in it. Herein lies salvation for this country.

Never has a single nation had the resources and opportunity to implement such thoughtfulness. The purity of the intent that would do so is not external to Divine Laws. Its scope is vast. For its virtue and goodness, all Universal Forces would stand behind it. We would no longer be working against the laws of creation, but replenishing the planet and protecting all that lives upon it.

CHAPTER FIFTEEN

15

GOODNESS WILL BRING PEACE TO THE EARTH

Intimation is like a seed. Everything that is created comes from the Thought of God, and then manifests into matter. A seed is as powerful as the Thought Itself, and therefore goes on. Not subject to time, it unfolds in its own way and extends what it is for millions of years.

A seed cannot grow if the air is not there. It needs the soil, the water, the sun, and the moon. An intimation also originates out of divine sources.

As more jobs are lost and unemployment looms like a gigantic monster, political systems are challenged. Politics all over the world now suffers from its own insecurity and falseness. Out of frustration, greed, and the desire for power, it disguises itself and resorts to war – which is quite profitable for some. Governments everywhere are spiritually barren, and national affairs are degenerating into crisis.

Transformation – so sorely needed – cannot occur when there is personal motive.

Politicians in most countries have become the enemies of their own people. They have no need to turn to virtuous values because compromises succeed without disturbing anyone. In a world of interpretation, everything can be justified, especially by the present media. Educated mindlessness is in charge via expedience and pretense. Is not our society becoming more and more regulated by fear, insecurity, and scarcity?

Disaster runs ahead of all solutions. Unemployment in America will be accompanied by a moral degeneration never heard of on such a large scale. Yet it need not be. The God-created world has enough resources for everyone.

Is it not we who impose limitations on a glorious world of abundance? What is lacking is discrimination between the God-created and the manmade – the Real and the unreal. The Real is Absolute; the unreal is man's projection.

To be consistent with the Will of God is religious. "In God We Trust." If this was so, this nation would know no unfulfillment. As an idea it has no meaning. To transcend the intellect is to know the sacredness and power of one's own will, which is not subject to fear. But we have built everything on a false premise. Why do we have resistance to unity and harmony?

The will has no traits of personality. It never wants nor seeks to achieve since it knows no unfulfillment.

In reality, the will undoes misperceptions and distortion. It is a cleanser of illusions. Intensified attention is awareness, the all-powerful will of man, one with God. Awareness has no activity in it. It is free of conflict and introduces man to his true, impersonal nature. Resistance and unwillingness to change are the issues. We want somehow to identify with our little self, remain preoccupied with "me and mine," and learn about self-improvement. Therefore, we depend on someone else telling us what to do.

Is this preoccupation not the very denial of one's own sacredness? God's will and man's will are one. What men and nations lack is compassion. The very realization of this truth could effortlessly turn the tide. How little we know of the power and purity of spontaneity that originates out of an unpressured moment of stillness in the mind of man. Stop a moment. See how detrimental most of man's external learning is now proving itself to be.

In true sharing one rises above sensation to the stillness of one's own being. Love knows the truth of service, for it extends the very Source of Life Itself. Everything else is of the relative level – this versus that. "LOVE YE ONE ANOTHER" intensifies love, when shared among human beings. Love is timeless and relates the human being to the vision of Reality behind appearance. There is no light in man's belief systems – be they political, economic, or religious – whereas the simplicity of a saint extends the kingdom of God on earth. He knows that nothing belongs to us – neither the earth, the tree, nor the water – and yet it is there to sustain life. We too, knowing this, would have reverence and contentment in our relationship with the universe. Having something to give we would be truly productive. Fulfillment does not seek and our lives would be a joy upon the earth. The presence of a holy person is a blessing.

Unemployment can be dealt with if we rise to meet the challenge. Humanism, having no lack, has the potentials. We need a shift of energy and interest within the nation – from vested interests to goodness. Man's compassion has infinite resources. Our thoughtfulness to extend goodwill to the "have nots" of the world would invoke divine forces to support us in freeing humanity from hunger. The change of objective is what is needed. Neither hunger nor unemployment are problems in reality. They only become problems when we lack goodness.

Man, in his goodness, is godlike. Peace and sanity will awaken him to the joy of his own impeccable Self. Obviously the insanity of fear opposes the Law of Love. Our justice, championing punishment, violates justice itself. The divine function of the human being is to extend Absolute Laws at the level of time and illusion. Only the wise, having overcome reaction and outgrown manmade, immature rules and concepts, can recognize the power of "turning the other cheek."

> As forgiveness allows love to return to my awareness, I will see a world of peace and safety and joy. [1]

What would remove wrong-mindedness in societies and nations? It would have to be a sense of responsibility in the individual willing to make internal corrections at the level of misperception. His own attention awakens potentials within and the power of his own will undoes self-deception. The awareness of his own sacredness introduces him to holy relationship, forever observant but free of judgment, with every living being. The ending of conflict within a small number of earnest people can transform the world.

Behold the insanity of our overly externalized world and its direction by which the individual is seduced and compelled to conform. Under the leadership of America since World War II, the military budget of most nations has skyrocketed, even in countries which hardly have enough food to eat. As long as war is profitable, how can there be peace in the world?

We have trillions of dollars for the destruction of mankind and nature but little money for food for the poorer nations. No wonder the country is under debt, inviting hunger to its own backdoor. These are the consequences of patronizing violence, dividing humanity, and extending lovelessness.

What could prevent America from destroying itself? Where would you start? What would you do with vested interests that do not want change, having worked all things in their own favor? Neither nationalism, nor the present economic system, nor those currently in power, foster change. At what point in loss of integrity does it become impossible for a nation to renew itself?

Nationalism is not a law; it is a lingering tribal idea of man. When the human being and his nations violate Eternal Laws, then there is unemployment, war, or earthquakes. We have polluted the atmosphere so much that we are close to seeing a shifting of the poles and vast earth changes around the globe.

The fanfare of affluence did not heighten human consciousness. Everything that we can do without spiritual awareness we have tried, and it does not work. We cannot ignore that we are of the spirit without having consequences. At present, any solution that refers to the loftiness and sacredness of the spirit is pronounced impractical; whatever keeps mankind wallowing in sensation is promoted. But there is no need for America to hit the bottom. Seen as a warning, unemployment could be a good thing. True prosperity comes not from our labors, but from right relationship with the earth.

With the advent of American supremacy, mankind entered an age of tremendous scientific development. America could still lead the world by directing her technology to the primary needs of humanity – food, shelter, clothing. This country could produce enough to feed the nations of the Third World.

First provide food for the people in these under-developed countries, and then help them revolutionize their own agricultural development. This would transform their economies, increase their ability to produce, and benefit America's agriculture and economy too.

The age of using bullock carts and wooden plows pulled by oxen is over. Having thousands of water pumps would make the land more productive. The

Food and Agriculture Organization (FAO) of the United Nations is fully familiar with what to do. It just needs to be supported. Could America come forth to do so? The know-how is there, but the help so far has not been in proportion to the need. There have been a lot of kind gestures – but now it has to be done on a vast scale. We have been trying to irrigate a field with a bucket of water.

In the early stages America could help get small projects in rural areas off the ground. It would require introducing the underdeveloped area to the industrial approach of mechanized farming. It is like lending a helping hand – starting with decentralized projects in remote areas so that they spread out and are not monopolized.

Each country could support its projects to its own capacity to begin with and pay for the equipment America provides at cost out of their new wealth. While there would be no profit in it, there would be no financial loss, either. The helper – America – could pay the salaries of its workers out of goodwill. Soldiers and sailors are already on salary, and could give themselves to service rather than to unemployment. They are well-organized and disciplined already, are used to doing what needs to be done, and know the resources of today's technology.

Once land is made productive and the primary needs of these nations are met, they would have the means to finance their own industries. This shift from aid to trade would help both America and the people who were once poor. The result would be a productive, ongoing relationship beneficial to the whole human race and a solution to unemployment at home.

Aid represents emergency measures and no country can rely upon it for long. The shift from aid to trade is miraculous. In trade, both nations prosper because the poorer nation can afford to buy equipment to industrialize its own country. Humanism works; replacing greed with goodness has more benefits than we realize.

After the Second World War, the population exploded. To a great extent prosperity itself would deal with the issue of population growth. This has already been demonstrated in Western societies.

A prosperous nation is responsible for extending harmonious goodwill. It is this thoughtfulness that gladdens the heart and leads to right relationship. Meeting the primary needs of man will energize this age. There is no reason why everyone in the world cannot be sheltered – owning his own home, even with a plot of land.

What is God's belongs to everyone,
and is his due. [2]

The challenge is to decentralize power, population, and wealth. Mere understanding is not good enough; it is a substitute for the Eternal Law.

The teachers of God have trust in the world,
because they have learned it is not governed
by the laws the world made up. It is governed

*by a Power That is in them but not of them. It
is this Power That keeps all things safe.* [3]

What is real is real forever. It does not change, for
Reality is part of Universal Laws. There is the Divine
Hand in what is timeless that nothing external can
affect. To goodness nothing is external, for it is Absolute.

Cruelty, problems, and deprivation arise as we
move from right relationship to expedience. It is this
that needs correction. The silent power of goodness
brings prosperity to mankind. It can change climates
and bring rain to a barren world. It is compassion that
is lacking, not food.

*All the help you can accept will be provided,
and not one need you have will not be met.* [4]

Universal forces accompany the movement towards unity and harmony. Each race has its own
intrinsic temperament, expression, and resources.
Each region should be allowed the space to prosper
and to flower in its own environment.

All resources are at the level of humanism. All
resources are at the level of Life.

When we are related to the Source of Life, we are
part of its abundance. Nationalism and other abstract
concepts and dogmas divide man and are largely the
cause of insecurity and poverty in the world. But in
Life there is no lack. In right thinking there is no lack.
Everything in nature gives, whether it is fragrance or
food. Rivers flow. The sun shines. There is the silent
purity of dew. Nature continues to replenish itself. Life

is sacred. Man's love for virtue and for the earth would change its vibration, and the stars would bless the happy planet below.

What we need to do is overcome self-imposed limitations. They are not of love or God; they are of the perversity of thinking that we learn in schools. There is no truth in them. It is time for us to outgrow immature thinking and be human beings rather than citizens attached to a flag. Nationalism produces no true leadership; it is an assumed, imposed authority based on a pretense.

Pretense is the wrong-mindedness that is taught everywhere. Harmony has its own potentials and is the fruit of goodness. We know little of the Love that sustains life or of Divine Intelligence. Is not falseness to oneself a curse? When will we ever awaken from *...the sleep of forgetfulness*[5] to realize our true Identity? How few are awakened from within.

There is an inherent joy within each one of us that lacks nothing, for it is forever grateful. Gratefulness has yet to sing its songs upon this planet. What are the resources of humanism? What in reality is true productivity and service? These are the questions we must ask.

Any solutions we pose for America will result in increased unemployment. Even though we have got ourselves trapped, transformation is always possible. But it demands a contact with self-honesty — the space within — that has the potential to cope with any challenge.

The human being is supreme in Creation. His potentials have no limitation. The action of transformation starts not with seeking but with the undoing of misperceptions and wrong-mindedness. The very problem becomes the solution. Is America willing to abolish war and end poverty upon the planet? If so, then right away we will have to more than double the production of food so that every living being has enough to eat. This would make right use of the technology we have, end the problem of unemployment, and feed the world!

Goodness has its own insight, a link with the universe. True productivity is oriented toward service rather than profit. But in that there is the true gain.

What would be required to make the rural areas of the world self-sufficient? The planet is in need of more vegetation. Growing more food would require roads, bridges, canals for irrigation, hydroelectric dams, and better seeds. It won't lead to the rich getting richer but to enriching mankind. The technology that would be necessary to accomplish this would no longer be wasteful but truly productive.

India was not producing enough food to feed all its people after achieving freedom, even though eighty-five percent of her population lived on the land. In fact, she imported millions of dollars worth of food annually. But the well-organized Rural Community Projects revolutionized agriculture, and in less than a decade, India was exporting food.

India learned that each acre of land could more than double its production, and that irrigating barren earth lets it contribute to the new wealth of a country. As prosperity comes, farmers are able to buy small-scale agricultural machinery. Millions of tractors and water pumps can be sold in tomorrow's world because better agricultural methods will be so desperately needed.

A humanistic approach harmonizes relationships. Reverence allows nature to be true to itself. Once war is abolished and the primary needs are met everywhere simultaneously, we will have ushered in the sanity of a new age upon this planet.

The problem is never external. Man's political systems of today are antiquated. His economic systems are corrupt. His educational systems are barren of ethics or morality. What works is the military. Its technology of destruction is unsurpassed. The outcome of a militaristic approach to life is predictable, for it is contrary to Divine Laws. A loveless practicality is strangling the nation. From the present perspective, in every direction America looks, disaster is around the corner.

Now it even seems the more prosperous a nation is, the more pressured and stimulated. "THE MEEK SHALL INHERIT THE EARTH" [6] is too profound a principle for the intellect to comprehend. It may well be that America cannot afford this new thinking and will hit bottom, for she lacks resilience and serenity. Vested interests have become the enemy. She is not aligned with Universal Laws.

Yet it is possible to rise to wisdom, and undo violence and self-destruction at home as well as abroad. Goodness opens a new vista for America and mankind where reverence and thoughtfulness take precedence. It will come about, whether or not America can rise to merit the opportunity. If she does not, other parts of the world will lead the way. No one can undermine the capacity of the human being. Every living person upon this planet has a precise function.

My part is essential
to God's plan for salvation. [7]

There is enough military equipment – vehicles and planes – to build a better world. Warships could transport food and machinery where they are needed. Jeeps, trucks, and even tanks could be converted initially to serve as tractors. The U.S. Navy could serve in transferring thousands of helpers to go abroad on their peaceful missions, and the sailors could stay for a given time in an area, survey the needs, and help with the building of the means for a new economy, industry, and management. Navy and Army officials could be instructed about the ways and means for carrying out the projects. With no profit or loss, all the information necessary from different quarters of the world could be accessible. That is especially important for governments of poorer nations which have limited understanding of the skills and equipment needed.

Overall, it is a vast project and undertaking. But in the beginning, and at the grassroots level, skills are even more important than costly equipment. One project mastered, or given attention, becomes the model. Once it is understood by American servicemen, they can pass it on to the local areas. It is working with the government and the people of each country – irrespective of their political or economic views, or racial background. The human being is seen as the human being, his belief systems representing his own traditions in which there is no need to interfere.

The personnel of hundreds of American warships could revolutionize a continent because their service would be based on goodwill – not business, or political or religious dogma. For the first time, man goes to help, not to sell or conquer or convert. It is like sharing a new technology, a new science of universal kindness – converting destructive warships to constructive uses. Going to serve rather than to destroy would heighten morality everywhere and transform Americans with its givingness. This action of sanity would help cleanse the heart of man of fear and hostility.

Productivity is basic. Survival depends on it. This relationship of caring could evolve into a world free of war. It would become America to initiate incentives for peace and humanism on the planet.

Such an action could transform the world within a few years – especially if America's heart were in it. Overnight, hundreds of hospitals and dispensaries could arise. Carpenters, potters, and bakers could be taught to produce more efficiently with laborsaving devices. It is important to help these people, but not to take their simplicity away.

We have to protect the underdeveloped areas of the Third World from imitating the overly externalized lifestyles of the West that limit human life to sensation. Sensationalism is an epidemic we need not export.

Resources for these peaceful missions are surely there. It will cost a lot less than the Vietnam and Iraqi Wars, yet it will be a lifesaver – for America, too. All that is needed is the same American enthusiasm and determination exhibited in the U.S. military action of Desert Storm in the Persian Gulf.

Other nations will join and support this noble cause. Reverence for life could be shared by the whole world – no matter what differences there are on other issues. Togetherness would harmonize relationships and lift human morale. America's destiny depends on it. America could be Joseph* for the lean years ahead.

Now that America is the only superpower, her only sane option is to support a war-free world. Otherwise she will destroy herself with domestic problems. Wastefulness has brought poverty to America's doorstep. The price of food could be so low! There is no need for a packet of carrots to cost more than a few cents.

In order to cope with the primary needs of man, we need to think impersonally. Limiting oneself is a contradiction. There is no scarcity where there is non-waste and simplicity. What is required is a total transformation in the premise of our thinking. Our very education needs to be revolutionized. The present system is primitive for the most part. Training the

---

* Joseph, a prophet of God in the Old Testament, prepared the Pharaoh in Egypt for the seven lean years. For more about Joseph refer to the Addenda, The Foundation For Life Action, pages 249-251.

brain never soars beyond the body cells. Instead, it stimulates ambition and selfishness. We need not be programmed to obey and to submit.

Education is to awaken the student's vast inner potentials, and not merely confine him to memory. Education, religion, and the politics of self-seeking are deluding mankind by limiting him to the world of appearance. We need to change our values and transform the educational system.

I will not value what is valueless. [8]

This can only be in effect when our education has undergone a renewal. That is the first step – to undo whatever assumes false reality and to question the abstract. Education must do more than turn out wage-earners. True education is a sharing where the light of miracles is present. It is not only teaching; it is more an inner awakening.

Our present educational system does not relate the human being to the underlying reality of his divine nature. The universe, when seen by the senses, limits us to appearances. We are often deceived by its outward aspect. Truth is beyond sense perception. Love is a state of being and not an activity of thought.

There is perfect order in the vast universe. Disorder is in the manmade world. Humanity is one. Therefore, the function of education is to relate us to this reality. In actuality there is no past or future – yet we are educated to trust in our distractions from the timeless Present.

Stillness is sacred and as vast as the Present. What is ever present and direct needs no education, only awareness. Nothing is comparable to the innocence of the silent mind of man, and of that we know hardly anything.

The real function of education is to connect us with reality and not to the names we give the world of appearances. Inner awakening requires going beyond the body senses, not personalizing life and limiting ourselves to physicality.

Life is divine. Perfection, in reality having no lack, need not be sought. It is so; there are no means to it. But the ability to recognize the truth of this is what is missing. We are so preoccupied with the fallacy of activity and self-improvement. The human being, when inconsistent with Divine Law, is detrimental to himself. In his unawareness he interferes with the source of his own being. In a recent letter received from Mother Teresa, she said: "Continue to pray ... that we may not spoil God's work."

True knowledge is of Eternal Laws. The absolute has no opposite to it. Truth or love or gratefulness or peace of mind or oneness of life cannot be understood by justifying interpretations.

Mass education has gone astray when it teaches *about* truth and not Truth Itself. Yes, we need to learn about our physical self and the physical world; but it is our attachment that brings disorder. Man is part of the perfect order of the universe. His nature is divine. The importance of,

"Know thyself"

cannot be underestimated, nor the wisdom of,

SEEK YE FIRST THE KINGDOM OF GOD,
AND HIS RIGHTEOUSNESS;
AND ALL THESE THINGS
SHALL BE ADDED UNTO YOU. [9]

Rightness seems difficult for most people, but it is simple. There is no complexity in truth. Non-compromise is a power in itself. This power is within each one of us. It is the vitality of truth and uncontaminated compassion. It is the way of love that gives, but wants nothing. The universe responds to the call of an uncompromising man. His integrity fits into no situations and will not conform to circumstances. The wise is not controlled by the external. Selflessness is non-dependent. It is a power in itself. The purity of motiveless life is blessed. Infinite blessing surrounds the unselfish.

The reversal process is from fear to love and goodness. The reversal process from politics to humanism is not an easy transformation to make only if there is resistance. Willingness within to allow rightness to extend will facilitate it. There is no lack of potential, only of goodwill.

It would not take any more ingenuity or funds than having to bear the vast expenditure for military bases around the globe in order to police the world. In reality these are not only unessential but detrimental. Alliances with corrupt dictators contradict every ethic.

The few that profit are even now a formidable force directing America's domestic affairs to their advantage. Money and power concentrated in the hands of the few is largely the source of America's downfall.

Mankind is caught in the problem of possessiveness and insecurity. In the end even the banking system may prove as unreliable as our calculating thoughts. What is reliable is the honest word. The word of goodness is like a seed that is ageless and is accessible to the ear that heeds.

There is much to be done in affluent America while it is still affluent. Urgency is the word. Celestial speedup is upon us. Unemployment, with its surplus workers and machinery, can serve a good purpose. The power of goodness will bring peace to this planet.

To discriminate between Eternal Laws and man-made rules requires an entirely different approach to life, not just another intellectual perspective. Abstract concepts, dogmas, ideas, and belief systems are man-made. They could be termed "educated ignorance," and there is no peace in them. What is Absolute is of God – eternal, changeless, without an opposite — and hence unaffected by anything external. Manmade rules are unreal.

My thoughts are images that I have made. [10]

All things I think I see reflect ideas. [11]

Goodness and gratefulness are eternal attributes of the spirit. Love and truth are Absolute and ever-present. Manmade rules are questionable, but mass education continues to ignore the human being's boundless spiritual potentials.

Awareness of Eternal Laws undoes manmade rules. This is a Law.

My only function is the one God gave me [12]

means that human being is not subject to the principle of cause and effect, or consequences. His real function is to journey toward truth, having faith in his own integrity, and live by righteousness — the Law at work in life.

We cannot ignore the significance of spiritual values. The discovery of perfection is not denied to man.
Spirit is in a state of grace forever. [13]

Man's real nature is divine. Seeing the fact as a fact liberates us. Peace is of the One Mind of God of which we are all a part.

Where there is integrity there can be no lack. All power is given to man through the Word that created him.

There is tremendous goodwill in America. As mankind moves closer to a life of the spirit, goodness will bring peace to the earth.

Your Will can do all things in me,
and then extend to all the world as well through me.
There is no limit on Your Will.
And so all power has been given to Your Son. [14]

CHAPTER SIXTEEN

16

"I AM UNDER NO LAWS BUT GOD'S."

THE QUESTION IS – how does the individual undo stimulation and dependence on the system in order to bring order in his own life? And what would it take to make the internal change, make contact with his own divinity, and be a part of Universal Laws? The function of a good society is to produce individuals who outgrow society. As Ralph Waldo Emerson said,

> "What lies behind us and before us are small matters, compared to what lies within us."

It is in America that a new beginning emerges with the advent of *A Course in Miracles. A Course In Miracles*, the first scripture to originate in English, has come to awaken man from ...*the sleep of forgetfulness,* [1] the illusion that life is external. It offers the Thoughts of God as a gift to all mankind. Every sentence of the Course dispels our misperceptions. It declares:

> *Nothing real can be threatened.*
> *Nothing unreal exists.*

Lesson 76 of the *Workbook For Students* reassures us:

> *"I am under no laws but God's."*

> *We have observed before how many senseless things have seemed to you to be salvation. Each has imprisoned you with laws as senseless as itself. You are not bound by them, yet to understand that this is so, you must first realize salvation lies not there. While you would seek for it in things that have no meaning, you bind yourself to laws that make no sense. Thus do you seek to prove salvation is where it is not....*

> *Think of the freedom in the recognition that you are not bound by all the strange and twisted laws you have set up to save you. You really think that you would starve unless you have stacks of green paper strips and piles of metal discs. You really think a small round pellet or some fluid pushed into your veins through a sharpened needle will ward off disease and death. You really think you are alone unless another body is with you.*

> *It is insanity that thinks these things. You call them laws, and put them under different names in a long catalogue of rituals that have no use and serve no purpose. You think you must obey the laws of medicine, of economics*

and of health. Protect the body, and you will be saved....

There are no laws except the laws of God. This needs repeating over and over, until you realize it applies to everything that you have made in opposition to God's Will.

Rightness is the strength that overrules one's desire to seek advantage and preference. Certainty follows, as one sees that integrity works. *A Course In Miracles* makes one aware that Life is compassionate. It is gratefulness that lifts man and introduces him to his own sacredness. There is nothing else to learn. The Course makes possible the connection with the humanism of our God-created Self.

The premise of the lifestyle of *A Course In Miracles* is of the spirit. In reality, one's holiness is what one shares with another because that is who one truly is.

As forgiveness allows love to return to my awareness, I will see a world of peace and safety and joy. [2]

When two people share, there is no lack. Having something of our own to give leads toward service rather than dependence on jobs. In service is our salvation from insecurity and fear of the future. When you are the cause, you affect the externals; when you are an effect, you are externalized. Humanism does not have a program; it merely changes a value within the psyche.

It is not possible to live by certainty and rightness without trust in God. Religion is not intellectual but a state of being upon which time cannot intrude. The Course refers to it in Lesson 48:

"There is nothing to fear."

> *The idea for today simply states a fact. It is not a fact to those who believe in illusions, but illusions are not facts. In truth there is nothing to fear. It is very easy to recognize this. But it is very difficult to recognize it for those who want illusions to be true.* [3]

Politics, economy, conventional religion, and institutional education are founded on the abstract world of thought. There is not the sacredness of integrity in it, nor is there loftiness in its nationalism and commerce. It encourages falseness rather than awakening us to our divine nature. Only a motiveless life is free of consequences, for it extends the state that knows no lack.

Before the glow of affluence dims and flickers away let us gladden the heart of humanity for we are One in Life. A new and powerful action can inspire this nation to shining greatness. To make peace, charity, and goodness real is not costly. Givingness has its own resources. Goodwill reverses the process of degeneration. There is no lack where there is moral strength to unleash the full force of humanism. And the urgency is compelling.

Humanism responds to another's need out of its own clarity. It works in every situation, and always has to give. It can end the abuse of men and nations because it sees that exploitation is based on false values. In togetherness we could all survive and meet the primary needs of all mankind.

When we move toward rightness, order, and inner awareness, benevolent forces are there to help us. Everything is really secondary to our own inner awakening, for only in awakening will we find our function. Each of us needs friendship with wisdom. This is what the world has lost. We must rise to the Love of God within us, to the remembrance that we are One.

When one is disillusioned with the externals, there is no choice but to find the strength within. Everything else will fail – but the potentials of one's own sacredness are boundless.

TRANSFORMATION

It happens suddenly. There is a Voice
That speaks one Word, and everything is changed.

You understand an ancient parable
That seemed to be obscure. And yet it meant
Exactly what it said. The trivial
Enlarge in magnitude, while what seemed large
Resumes the littleness that is its due.
The dim grow bright, and what was bright before
Flickers and fades and finally is gone.
All things assume the role that was assigned
Before time was, in ancient harmony
That sings of Heaven in compelling tones
Which wipe away the doubting and the care
All other roles convey. For certainty
Must be of God.
                        It happens suddenly,
And all things change. The rhythm of the world
Shifts into concert. What was harsh before
And seemed to speak of death now sings of life,
And joins the chorus to eternity.
Eyes that were blind begin to see, and ears
Long deaf to melody begin to hear.
Into the sudden stillness is reborn
The Ancient singing of creation's song,
Long silenced but remembered. By the tomb
The angel stands in shining hopefulness
To give salvation's message: "Be you free,
And stay not here. Go on to Galilee."*

---

* From *The Gifts of God* by Dr. Helen Schucman (Foundation for Inner Peace, 1982), page 64.

243

ADDENDA

THE FOUNDATION
FOR LIFE ACTION

LIFE IS TOO VAST, timeless, and whole for the brain to grasp. Whenever one has some glimpse of its sacredness, attention intensifies and brings us to silence. We have to silence our brains to go beyond the world of appearances; thought has to cease in order to be with what is ever-present and unchangeable – the Christ that the human being is. Until we make that contact our real work has not begun and, in one way or another, the issue of survival consumes our energy.

But when, with the Grace of God, something else is awakened within, you begin to care for everyone and everything you see. One gets a glimpse that in moments of wholeness there is not the separation. As you begin to undo fragmentation in yourself – the way in which the brain separates – another action commences of which you may not be fully conscious. When this awakening starts to dawn, you begin to value miracles, the involuntary Action of Life. The learning phase is over and the unlearning of everything that blocks contact with truth begins.

A new action was born in me with the advent of *A Course In Miracles*. This is the experiment at the Foundation for Life Action in Los Angeles, California, a school to train students to bring *A Course In Miracles* into application. Through our work, eternal principles have been discovered to serve mankind in times ahead. This experiment belongs to all generations. To the degree it is impersonal, to the degree it is wise, it needs to be known.

The work of the Foundation for Life Action began as I was guided internally to give workshops and retreats. I was told, "Put away your false modesty. You are a teacher in your own right."

When something is authentic, it is always one-to-one with the serious few. And it is non-commercial. The focus of attention is basic and an intimate atmosphere essential. Like the dialogues of the Upanishads or of Socrates and Plato, it allows for the sharing of something unknown.

Our action started in a small way. We insisted upon self-reliance and the commandment Mr. Krishnamurti gave to me: "Never take advantage of another." This eliminated dependence on the externals, for we refused to accept charity or ask for donations, and directed our energies toward finding the treasure within ourselves.

The small group that stayed on after the One Year Non-Commercialized Retreat: A Serious Study of *A Course In Miracles*, held during 1983-1984, [1] became part of the Foundation for Life Action and the nucleus of the school to train students to bring the Course into application.

A clairvoyant said of the One Year Retreat: "It is a process of inner selection, one of the golden opportunities on the planet. But who is ready? It has to be an inner calling, for that is the level at which the transformation will take place." Dr. Elisabeth Kubler-Ross, the physician known for her work on death and dying, said: "Those who emerge from the One Year Retreat will be self-reliant and dependable in crisis and catastrophe."

Self-reliance requires productive and intrinsic work. To come to self-reliance the students began transcribing tapes from the One Year Retreat. They felt that what had helped them could also help others; and so, they made the material available in books and audiotapes.

During a trip to England in 1988, I was directed internally to bring the hearts of all my blood relatives to gladness. I was being introduced to the action of completion in order to merit a motiveless life free of consequences. While in London, Joseph's Plan was intimated to me.

Joseph, a prophet of God in the Old Testament, [2] prepared the Pharaoh in Egypt for the seven lean years. The story is given in the Bible so that we may learn to be responsible because this pattern repeats itself throughout the centuries.

Time Magazine reported: "In Biblical times, a famed Pharaoh once dreamed of seven fat years of plenty followed by seven lean years of want. With the United States economy in the seventh year of a record peace time expansion, signs are multiplying that for many Americans, the fat times are coming to an end. At the moment, no Joseph is available to persuade

Washington to adopt frugal habits, even when the fat years are in danger of turning to lean ones."*

Joseph was a man who knew nothing of greed or fear. He extended who he was as God created him. In his wholeness, he intensified all men for all time. Such is Joseph, the prophet of God. This unseparated, eternal man inspired me with his pure abundance. In his stillness there was no opposite. Joseph was wholly himself. He always acted out of awareness. In truth, Joseph represents a state of celibacy, a life free of karma.

Spontaneously, his goodness and his sense of wholeness focused the rays of the Kingdom on earth. Yet in the world of time, this man of Divine Intelligence was falsely accused and cast into prison. Joseph had no revenge, no reaction. His honesty set him free to do God's Will. From Joseph we can learn that in the acceptance of Divine Will, man's life becomes selfless and impersonal.

The Pharaoh, whose dream Joseph interpreted, was a noble and farsighted king – one to whom the human being was important, not politics. The pharaohs, in their uninterrupted space, built the enduring and mysterious pyramids. It is likely that within the pyramid are held man's innermost vibrations which transcend the manifested world of appearances.

The Pharaoh had the discrimination of a true ruler and, in his heart, the kindness of a king for his people. His trust and courage made him an eternal king in the memory of men for all time. When the Pharaoh first met Joseph, there stood before him a man who had never

---

* May 22, 1989 issue.

told a lie. The Pharaoh, attentive yet serene, recognized Joseph from the strength of his certainty, which effortlessly extended the power of the Will. Stop for a moment and imagine: What must Joseph's voice have been like? Intensity of silence surrounded him. The Pharaoh saw that one who lives by Eternal Laws is a law unto himself.

Hearing Joseph's true words, the Pharaoh placed no conditions. He knew that a law does not compromise. Joseph had something to give and the wise Pharaoh responded with giving as well. That is the meeting ground of togetherness.

We need to know that true words leave their light behind for all generations to come. Thus what has once occurred need never victimize us again. Joseph's incorruptibility is now our strength. One's own attention is all-wise and ever resourceful. We can learn from Joseph and the Pharaoh how to prepare and how to relate with Universal Forces.

There is never lack in the wholeness of creation. Thus, the issue is always one of internal correction. Deprivation and scarcity are misperceptions; they are self-imposed.

Behold the example of the Pharaoh of generous heart and trust in goodness, who avoided the crisis by recognizing a man of awakened intelligence and impersonal life. The Pharaoh demonstrated that for both the state and the individual, transformation is possible.

On reading about Joseph, I was charged. It was not enthusiasm, nor anything necessarily mental. The direction was given. In my case it started in 1989 with the offering of a Forty Days Retreat in New Mexico. Over one hundred and ten participants attended. In addition, many other shorter retreats were subsequently offered around the country. The income from all of these retreats has been put aside for Joseph's Plan. It is entrusted to be used to meet the primary needs of mankind.

It is more than a joy to keep Joseph's Plan impeccable. What a blessing to know that ordinary people can be purified by the work they do when the Grace of God accompanies it. Nothing is as precious as selflessness that slowly purifies one's mind and spirit with the boon of service. I can truthfully say it is not I who is selfless. Selflessness is beyond the realm of words. But the Grace of God is miraculous. It can make the lame walk and the blind see. What is at work in all of this is the energy of Gratefulness.

Looking back, it is marvelous how Life prepared us with having our own intrinsic work; being detached and owning no property; and discovering the strength of rightness inherent in self-reliance. Until you have found your own voice, your own dignity, it is not possible to merit service. Now we are blessed with the sacredness of Joseph's Plan, which is the fulfillment of having something to give. When what you give is the Given, you are an extension of Joseph's Plan. [3]

Joseph, the servant of God, lives by faith for he knows that whatever anyone does externally is not of God. The external can put you in prison but it cannot disturb your peace.

As long as we live by thought, nothing we say is true. Everyone wants to do good but that good may not be sensitive. Good is absolute; it is not of personality. The goodness of God sensitizes you to another person's need and it is your joy to meet it. When you care, you heed another's words so intensely that your own interpretation and opinion are silenced. Then you qualify to be the blessed servant of God. Just by listening, you will know what to do and what to impart. To be the blessed servant is to know certainty. You receive what the other needs and bring light into confusion and darkness. In the world of insight there is the pure healing because you are not opposing the Will of God.

The blessed servant of God must live by Universal Laws. That is his preparation. Cleansed of relative knowledge, he purifies his speech and masters communication. He is ever aware of the divine action in his life. Order is needed to have the space and capacity to maintain the light that surrounds him.

Swami Brahmananda, one of Sri Ramakrishna's foremost disciples said that one becomes truly entitled to work only after God-realization. He shared that in the joy of samadhi the world vanishes, and that peace comes by loving God and having true faith in Him. The one who is calculating would be lost.

*Today we will receive instead of plan
that we may give instead of organize.* [4]

Our experiment is not only to outgrow organization but also to bring fruit to the altar. [5] The servants of God need the energy of love in order to receive. They will go out in this chaotic world, having established this capacity to receive, and then it will be their own direct light and extension. The servants will be blessed with faith. They could be in the midst of earthquakes and fire and nothing could touch them.

Five or six years ago, I had an intimation that our work would one day become linked with that of Mother Teresa. It was a clear realization at a different level of being. It is interesting to see how long it takes for something to manifest and become implemented at this level. The more one leaves it alone, the more impersonal it is and, therefore, the more sacred. That is the way it is meant to be. This is easier said than done, however. In one way or another, we always interfere.

When Charles Johnson and I travelled to India in 1989, we visited Mother Teresa's Missionaries of Charity in Calcutta. The words on the altar of their little chapel, "I THIRST," [6] silenced me through and through. Mother Teresa was not well, so we met with Sister Priscilla who was in charge. She said to us, "We don't want money. We need people with hearts to give and lives to serve." At the time I told Sister Priscilla that I believed there were those among us in Los Angeles who would be interested. She recommended that we contact Sister Sylvia who was responsible for the missions in the western part of the United States.

A letter was sent to Sister Sylvia upon our returning to California. Shortly thereafter, Sister Angelina, the Superior of the Lynwood Mission near Los Angeles, called and shared with us ways in which volunteers could help. She also made it clear that although active involvement was not necessary, prayers would be appreciated.

The Sisters provide a home for unwed mothers in Lynwood, about thirty-five minutes from the Foundation. We began sending two people for several hours every Saturday. There was gardening, sewing, carpentry, and other miscellaneous tasks to do. Sometimes we helped in preparing grocery bags of donated food items for the needy. One of the Sisters told us that they had been praying for someone to help with the work just before we came to offer our services. They were grateful and acknowledged the Hand of the Lord in answering this prayer. Our blessing was in making the commitment to come on a regular basis.

When our volunteers return from the Mission, they are always inspired by the atmosphere there. It is most refreshing to see that there is no judgment on the Sisters' part regarding the unwed mothers. What these Sisters must have imbibed from Mother Teresa that allowed them to totally respond to what she herself had seen – the Light of the Christ in the human being. It takes nine or more years to go through the training. But just that one would take nine years to come to inner awakening and this sharing of life speaks of the quality of the Sisters. It is not impulsive. Not many people would last nine years unless their calling were authentic.

Our students, on returning from the Lynwood Mission, have remarked that it is as if their hands are blessed in doing the work. What a remarkable discovery, the blessing of service. You exist for your brother and, out of that love, you work. Our volunteers were also affected by the uncomplicated and unsentimental approach of the Sisters. It is obvious that they are "about their Father's business." [7] There is warmth and joy, but they do not have the space for idle conversation or gossip.

When we discovered that they often do not have enough food to give to the poor, we committed ourselves to donating $50 a week for one year. We met as a group and discussed the value of being consistent in giving. We wanted to offer an amount that would allow others, too, to be a part of the program and receive the gift of being in contact with their work. The donation is used to purchase bulk food – hundred pound sacks of flour, beans, sugar, oats, powdered milk, etc. – to add to their limited food supply for weekly distribution to the poor.

We wrote to Mother Teresa in India thanking her for providing the inspiration and the means by which we could assist in the work of meeting basic needs of our brothers. Mother Teresa wrote:

> "Thank you for your warm letter and the kind sentiments you have expressed in it. How beautiful it is to know that you all have allowed your lives to be touched by the presence of Jesus in the poor. He keeps using the poor to draw us all together. In allowing us to serve them and in accepting our service, the poor draw the best out of us, or rather, it is Jesus using the poor, Who makes us the sunshine of His love and compassion with them.

"In the measure we allow God to empty us of self and pride, we enable Him to fill us with His love so we may seek to give more than to receive, to serve rather than be served. Let us pray for all at the Foundation for Life Action that they may make the prayer of St. Francis their own and live it in seeking to love rather than to be loved.

"The Fruit of Silence is Prayer.
The Fruit of Prayer is Faith.
The Fruit of Faith is Love.
The Fruit of Love is Service.
The Fruit of Service is Peace."

Dr. Helen Schucman, the Scribe of *A Course In Miracles*, had said to me: "Send the world your love. It will come back to you." Mother Teresa's work best exemplifies this statement. When I asked Dr. Schucman if there was anyone who really lived *A Course In Miracles* in our time, she replied that Mother Teresa was one. Mother Teresa is not distracted by the abstract world of ideas. Hers is the energy of love and compassion which knows no lack. She is always present with what she is doing, for her life and God's Will are not in contradiction.

On my first visit to meet Sister Angelina, after our students had gone to volunteer for more than a year, she told me that her Sisters never knew such faces existed in the outside world as those of the young people at the Foundation. She also said that our presence at their Mission was a strength and an inspiration to the Sisters. When I asked Sister Angelina whether there were other projects which we could support, she thought for awhile and then said, "No, we have no needs." Now that is very simple.

Stop for a moment and consider what this means. They have no needs because they don't believe in the future. They know for certain that tomorrow will take care of itself and they have enough for today. It is a different language. When you really hear it, your conflict ends also. Their authenticity introduces you to a moment of wholeness.

We were blessed to become related with the Missionaries of Charity in Lima, Peru, on my visit there in the Fall of 1990. We were told by the Sisters that on many days there was a shortage of bread. When we wrote to Mother Teresa inquiring whether we could establish bakery facilities in the Mission, she responded that she did not want her Sisters to get involved in a bakery.

In this statement one discovers the principles upon which her work is based. It is always related to an extension of the Will and compassion of God which provides. It is an action of faith and truth which only knows abundance. How inspiring this is. Mother Teresa and her Sisters have no sense of scarcity because they are the blessed servants of God. I wrote to Mother Teresa:

> "...We see such wisdom in your not getting the Sisters involved in the organization of a bakery. Your love for poverty and simplicity is a strength and a guidance to us.

"We have been a witness to the work at the Mission here in Lynwood with which we have close contact. Our group goes and volunteers services once or twice a week regularly, and they come back beaming. We are also inspired by the work being done by the Sisters at Misioneras de la Caridad in Lima, Peru, and we are responding to some of the needs there with gladness in our heart.

"We have what is called Joseph's Fund to meet the primary needs of man. It is to be kept impeccable, since it is entrusted by the Lord. We have dedicated two years to the service of Joseph Plan and now there are substantial funds.

"What we would like to ask is that if any project in any of the Missions of Charity needs financial help, would you please let us know so that we may participate in it? We speak in an impersonal way; the funds are meant to meet the primary needs of man during the lean years.

"The Joseph Plan demands integrity and I pray daily, 'Lord, prevent me from making a mistake.' May your blessings and prayers be upon it."

Mother Teresa responded:

"I pray for you and for all at the Foundation for Life Action that you be God's Hands to serve the poor and His Heart to love the poorest of the Poor. Since God has already entrusted you with substantial funds set up a project yourselves so you may bring hope into the lives of those on the brink of despair through your service. Since you are interested in helping the poor, be fully involved in doing something concrete for them. I thank you for your kind interest in our works of love and for your thoughtful and generous offer.

God bless you,
Mother Teresa"

Since receiving this letter, we have come to a unanimous decision. We see the rightness of disbanding the organization of the Foundation for Life Action by Easter, 1992, after having been together for nine years.

The Foundation has been a school to train students of *A Course In Miracles* to be productive and self-reliant, having something of their own to give. The Foundation was not to seek results, but to value what is intrinsic. Primarily, laws and principles have been shared with the students rather than concepts. Inner transformation is not possible at the level of mere teaching and learning of ideas and ideals.

Several years ago, we recognized that, ultimately, having one's own intrinsic work and not working for another were essential to be consistent with the lifestyle of *A Course In Miracles*. We have realized a life of service is intrinsic and free from the conflict of external thought pressures. The issue of self-survival limits one to the insecurity of personalized life.

Knowing that a motiveless life is free of consequences, the premise of the Foundation, from its very
outset, has been not to be under obligation. People
sent us money and offered us properties which we
refused to accept because we did not feel a sense of
lack. Our needs were always met. For us, the human
being came first. We were determined never to expand
the group beyond thirty students.

We have established a rapport with Mother
Teresa's Missionary Sisters of Charity over the last
two years. This has been most helpful. It is our
dependability that has inspired closeness with the
Sisters. They value our consistency.

The Foundation has provided years of one-to-one
relationship, free of tuition, to prepare the students
to realize that enthusiasm and sentimentality have
little meaning in truth. Without dissolving the
abstract and interpretations, it is not possible to be
responsible for what you say or what you do.

The Sisters are a living example and their nine
years of preparation directly with Mother Teresa
herself have transformed their inner lives and related
each one to values of eternal and selfless life. What
the Sisters now extend is the natural goodness
awakened within themselves. It is no longer work but
an internal expression of their love for God.

Mother Teresa imparted Faith to her Sisters. When
you have Faith, you lack nothing. The Sisters never
seek, knowing fully well that God provides. They live
consistent with what the Prophet Isaiah said, "Keep
calm and be confident." Thus, they have the space

within their minds to see the Light of God that shines in "the poorest of the poor." The application of Truth in their lives brings to our attention the joy of LOVE YE ONE ANOTHER.

The Foundation has taken many steps to introduce our group to Mother Teresa's work and values. Now we send students from the Foundation, two-by-two, to spend an extended period of a week or a month in active participation with the Sisters at their Tijuana Mission. By the time Easter comes everyone will have gone through the actual experience of what constitutes service, or what is entailed in loving a brother more than yourself. It is challenging – the work of cleaning, scrubbing, washing people who are ill, nursing the abandoned, the poorest of the poor. But everyone at the Foundation is eager to go, and they come back inspired for having found some joy that was dormant within themselves.

At the end of November, 1991, we were told that Mother Teresa was likely to visit the West Coast sometime in December. Because of the evolving closeness over the last two years with the volunteers from the Foundation, the Sisters invited us to join with them in making contact with her. Arrangements were made for the students committed to service to meet with Mother Teresa. And on December 13, 1991, the meeting took place in Tijuana.

Time stopped. There was no haste or pressure. It was a meeting of life with Life, spacious, and with moments of perfection in the Now. I presented *A Course In Miracles* to Mother Teresa and asked that she bless the seventeen students committed to service. She blessed each one.

The students are indebted to the Foundation for the preparation that has introduced them to a different way of life. They are grateful, also, to close the Foundation and to stand on their own feet. Without detachment, man is a slave of the world.

Gratefulness is a power. Its spirit makes it possible for us to bring the external activity to an end without residue. We are all enriched for having witnessed the Hand of God in what we had undertaken to do and complete. During the nine years we never violated thoughtfulness; everyone has always been included in making decisions. Giving another the space for honesty is what made things work. This promoted a spirit of harmony and we have been blessed by it.

Our decision to disband the organization of the Foundation is an action similar to that of the Essenes of Jesus' time who, having completed their work, knew when to stop, and disappear. The Foundation for Life Action has succeeded in providing different values, virtue, and ethics in life.

My instruction to each one at the Foundation has been: Be true to yourself. If you stay together after the closing, the One Mind of the group will attract Universal Forces to you because of your dedication to service. Those who have given their lives to ...*removing the blocks to the awareness of Love's presence,* [8] will be energized and protected by Divine Laws.

God indeed can be reached directly, for there
is no distance between Him and His Son. His
awareness is in everyone's memory, and His
Word is written on everyone's heart. Yet this
awareness and this memory can arise across
the threshold of recognition only where all
barriers to truth have been removed....All the
help you can accept will be provided, and not
one need you have will not be met. [9]

Our non-commercialized experiment to bring *A Course In Miracles* into application in each student's life is a statement to everyone that the Grace of God is the Source of life and that newness is accessible. What the group will do will be their own creative expression. It may have no resemblance to Mother Teresa's work or to that of the Foundation, for how can you limit the glory of life to the bondage of the known. The new must always be free of the projections of goals.

A Course In Miracles embodies a power independent of the externals. It has its own resources and Divine Intelligence. The Course was published without the help of a traditional publisher and 750,000 copies have been sold without any formal advertising or promotion. At our relative level, the action of *A Course In Miracles* will continue to extend itself.

From its inception, the Foundation for Life Action, rooted in the sharing of *A Course In Miracles*, has stayed with self-reliance. It endeavors to remain non-commercial, having something to give.

The Foundation's first expression was through weekend workshops, followed by ten-day retreats.

These resulted in a forty-day residential retreat in 1981. *A Course In Miracles,* having 365 lessons, one for each day of the year, finally led the Foundation to offer the first One Year Non-Commercialized Retreat in the Course's history, as well as in the history of the New World. The One Year extended for nine years, and now the Foundation dissolves its organization.

The students present have discovered that the mania of personal wanting, with all its tribulation, can only be dissolved when one has realized the wisdom of giving. There is no peace in wanting. Joy is in the giving; and moral strength lies in meeting the needs of another. Freedom from wanting comes naturally when one realizes all needs are met by Life's Divine Intelligence.

Now everyone in the group is determined not to work for another or become a mercenary. It is this conviction that leads one to the life of service. The students must evolve to stand on their own feet and give expression to the awakened goodness in themselves. The Foundation school, having completed its work, closes.

All things are completed in detachment.

Life is Impersonal. Until one realizes the truth of this, the survival issue is not resolved. The personal cannot end anything; and its meaningless activity continues its involvement with the past. Ending is internal. It lets the joyous and the peaceful BE. The State of the Living Present reveals:

My mind is part of God's. I am very holy. [10]

The next action emerging is the Joseph Plan, which is Impersonal. It remains to be seen how it will unfold. The Joseph Plan is endowed with substantial funds, and there are twenty-two blessed servants of God who have taken a vow to give their lives to service and not be subject to anything external.

Each student could be a civilizing factor wherever he goes, and spontaneously respond in his own area to the need of another. The Joseph Plan will extend simultaneously in different places with the precept of *A Course In Miracles:*

To have, give all to all. [11]

*What is God's belongs to everyone,
and is his due.* [12]

REFERENCES

Chapter One: THE CITY AND LONELINESS

1. One of the Ten Commandments. See Deuteronomy 5:17.
2. Babylon, the metropolis of Chaldea, was known in the Bible for its grandeur and decadence.
3. "In God We Trust" appears to have been inspired by a line from *The Star Spangled Banner*, "In God is our trust," written by Francis Scott Key in 1814. "In God We Trust" first appeared on the coinage of the United States in 1864, during the presidency of Abraham Lincoln. It became the official motto of the United States in 1956. (Editor)

Chapter Two: HUMAN CONTACT BRINGS ABOUT THE "NEW"

1. Mr. Jiddu Krishnamurti (1895-1986) was a world renowned teacher and philosopher. (Editor)
2. As quoted in *Guru Nanak And The Origins Of The Sikh Faith* by Harbans Singh (Asia Publishing House, 1969).
3. *A Course In Miracles* (ACIM), first published in 1976 by the Foundation for Inner Peace, Glen Ellen, California, is a contemporary scripture which deals with the psychological/spiritual issues facing man today. It consists of three volumes: *Text* (I), *Workbook For Students* (II), and *Manual For Teachers* (III). The *Text*, 622 pages, sets forth the concepts on which the

thought system of the Course is based. The *Workbook For Students*, 478 pages, is designed to make possible the application of the concepts presented in the *Text* and consists of three hundred and sixty-five lessons, one for each day of the year. The *Manual For Teachers*, 88 pages, provides answers to some of the basic questions a student of the Course might ask and defines many of the terms used in the *Text*. (Editor)

Chapter Three: FROM THE CITY TO THE VEDIC AGE OF SHINING BEINGS EXTENDING THE WILL OF GOD

1. ACIM, II, page 126.
2. Refers to Noah, the Old Testament patriarch who, at God's command, built an ark that saved him, his family, and every kind of animal from the Great Flood. See Genesis, Chapters 5-10.

Chapter Four: THE HUMAN CRISIS – THE GAP IS INCREASING

1. The one commandment given by Jesus, "Love ye one another," appears many times in the New Testament. See, for example: John 13:34-35, 15-12, 15:17; Romans 13:8.
2. ACIM, II, page 23.
3. Refers to the Lord's Prayer from the Sermon on the Mount. See Matthew 6:10.

Chapter Five: AMERICA'S DESTINY

1. Swami Rama Tirtha was an Indian professor and mathematician who visited the United States in the early part of this century. For a discussion of Swami Rama Tirtha's influence on his life, see Tara Singh's *Awakening A Child From Within* (Life Action Press, 1990), pages 288-291. (Editor)
2. *Diet For A New America* by John Robbins (Stillpoint Publishing, 1987), pages 33 and 316.
3. Op. cit., pages 326, 329, and 326 respectively.

Chapter Six: AFFLUENCE WITHOUT WISDOM IS SELF-DESTRUCTIVE

1. *Love: A Fruit Always In Season – Daily Meditations* by Mother Teresa (Ignatius Press, 1987), page 228.

Chapter Eight: THE FUTURE OF MANKIND

1. ACIM, I, page 285.
2. In 1991 the United States lost a total of nearly 450,000 factory jobs. See *Facts On File*, January 16, 1992, page 21F3.
3. Swami Vivekananda as quoted in *The Dedicated; A Biography Of Nivedita* by Lizelle Reymond (John Day Company, 1953), page 43. Vivekananda (1863-1902) was the direct disciple cf Shri Ramakrishna and brought Vedanta to the West.
4. *Grunch of Giants* by R. Buckminster Fuller (St. Martin's Press, 1983), pages 1-2, 17 & 36.
5. Swami Vivekananda, op. cit., page 47.
6. ACIM, II, pages 277-279.

Chapter Nine: WHY HAS THERE ALWAYS BEEN WAR IN THE WORLD?

1. ACIM, I, page 452.
2. ACIM, II, page 185.
3. Matthew 5:44; Luke 6:27.
4. John 3:6.
5. Matthew 6:10.

Chapter Ten: THE NEW AGE

1. ACIM, I, pages 602-603.
2. Ancient Greek commandment written on the temple of Apollo in Delphi.

Chapter Eleven: DARK FORCES

1. ACIM, I, page 54.
2. ACIM, II, page 159.
3. ACIM, II, page 103.
4. ACIM, II, page 101.
5. ACIM, II, page 105.
6. ACIM, II, page 125.

7. ACIM, II, page 101.
8. ACIM, II, page 125.
9. ACIM, II, page 162.
10. ACIM, II, page 157.
11. ACIM, II, page 158.
12. ACIM, II, page 159.
13. ACIM, III, page 82.

Chapter Twelve: THE FORCES THAT SWAY HUMANITY

1. ACIM, II, page 126.
2. Refers to: "The peace of God, which passeth all understanding." See Philippians 4:7.
3. J. Krishnamurti, *Commentaries on Living, Third Series* (The Theosophical Publishing House, 1960), page 97.
4. Refers to "...whosoever shall smite thee on thy right cheek, turn to him the other also." See Matthew 5:39.

Chapter Thirteen: THE STILL MIND IS NOT SWAYED

1. ACIM, I, page 109.
2. *Nothing real can be threatened. Nothing unreal exists.* appears in the Introduction of the *Text* of *A Course In Miracles*. The complete Introduction reads:
This is a course in miracles. It is a required course. Only the time you take it is voluntary. Free will does not mean that you can establish the curriculum. It means only that you can elect what you want to take at a given time. The course does not aim at teaching the meaning of love, for that is beyond what can be taught. It does aim, however, at removing the blocks to the awareness of love's presence, which is your natural inheritance. The opposite of love is fear, but what is all-encompassing can have no opposite.
This course can therefore be summed up very simply in this way:
    Nothing real can be threatened.
    Nothing unreal exists.
Herein lies the peace of God.
3. As quoted by Plato in *Crito* (49d), translated by Hugh Tredennick, *The Collected Dialogues of Plato* (Princeton University Press, 1961), pages 34-35.

4. Luke 9:60.

Chapter Fourteen: COMING EVENTS CAST THEIR
SHADOW

1. *Indira Gandhi: Letters To An American Friend* written
   to Dorothy Norman (Harcourt Brace Jovanovich,
   1985). page 121.
2. Op. cit..
3. As quoted in *Memoirs Of Hope; Renewal And
   Endeavor* by Charles de Gaulle (Simon & Schuster,
   1971), page 256.
4. As quoted in *The Legacy Of Nehru*, edited by K.
   Natwar-Singh (John Day Company, 1965), page 107.
5. de Gaulle, op. cit., page 262.
6. From an article entitled, "Outlook 1992 - State Of The
   Union," *U.S. News & World Report*, Volume 111,
   Number 27, December 30, 1991, page 38.
7. From an interview of Indira Gandhi by Peter Jennings
   on ABC's "Issues and Answers," approximately 1966.
8. From a poem by Rainer Maria Rilke.

Chapter Fifteen: GOODNESS WILL BRING PEACE TO THE
EARTH

1. ACIM, II, page 89.
2. ACIM, I, page 503.
3. ACIM, III, page 8.
4. ACIM, III, page 62.
5. An excerpt from a prayer in *A Course In Miracles*, I,
   page 326: *Forgive us our illusions, Father, and help
   us to accept our true relationship with You, in which
   there are no illusions, and where none can ever enter.
   Our holiness is Yours. What can there be in us that
   needs forgiveness when Yours is perfect? The sleep of
   forgetfulness is only the unwillingness to remember
   Your Forgiveness and Your Love. Let us not wander
   into temptation, for the temptation of the Son of God is
   not Your Will. And let us receive only what You have
   given, and accept but this into the minds which You
   created and which You love. Amen.*
   This prayer has been referred to as *A Course In
   Miracles'* version of the Lord's Prayer. See: *Journey*

Without Distance: The Story Behind A Course In Miracles by Robert Skutch (Celestial Arts, 1984), page 68. This prayer is discussed in great detail in *Dialogues On A Course In Miracles* by Tara Singh (Life Action Press, 1987), pages 35-167. (Editor)
6. Psalm 37:11.
7. ACIM, II, page 177.
8. ACIM, II, page 239.
9. Matthew 6:33.
10. ACIM, II, page 25.
11. ACIM, II, page 454.
12. ACIM, II, page 107.
13. ACIM, I, page 7.
14. ACIM, II, page 450.

Chapter Sixteen: "I AM UNDER NO LAWS BUT GOD'S."

1. ACIM, II, page 89.
2. ACIM, II, page 77.

Addenda
THE FOUNDATION FOR LIFE ACTION

1. The One Year Non-Commercialized Retreat: A Serious Study of *A Course In Miracles* with Tara Singh took place in Los Angeles, California, from Easter Sunday, April 3, 1983 to Easter Sunday, April 22, 1984 with 50 participants from all over the United States. The years and events which led up to the One Year Retreat are documented in Tara Singh's *The Voice That Precedes Thought* (Life Action Press, 1987). Tara Singh's work with *A Course In Miracles* centers around his one-to-one relationship with a small number of serious students. This work is sponsored by the Foundation for Life Action. Mr. Singh has shared about his relationship with the Course and the Foundation for Life Action in each of his books. These excerpts provide a fascinating tapestry of the years from 1983-1992:
Preface to *A Course In Miracles – A Gift For All Mankind*, pages xiii-xvi.
Introduction to *Commentaries On A Course In Miracles*, pages xiv-xx.

Preface to *The Voice That Precedes Thought*, pages xvii-xviii.
Introduction to *Dialogues On A Course In Miracles*, pages 20-31.
The School – "*Having The Ears To Hear*," published in *Dialogues On A Course In Miracles*, pages 339-365.
Introduction to *How To Raise A Child Of God*, pages 39-42.
Introduction to the second edition of *How To Learn From A Course In Miracles*, pages 15-27.
Introduction to "*Nothing Real Can Be Threatened*," pages 11-27.
Autobiography in "*Nothing Real Can Be Threatened*, pages 255-262.
Addenda in *Awakening A Child From Within*, pages 377-378, 387, and 389-391. (Editor)
2. See Genesis 37 and following.
3. For further discussion of Joseph's Plan, see:
Introduction to Tara Singh's "*Nothing Real Can Be Threatened*" (Life Action Press, 1989), pages 24-27.
Addenda in *Awakening A Child From Within* (Life Action Press, 1991), pages 379-381 and 391. (Editor)
4. ACIM, II, page 248.
5. John 15:16.
6. John 19:28.
7. Luke 2:49.
8. ACIM, I, Introduction.
9. ACIM, III, pages 61-62.
10. ACIM, II, page 53.
11. ACIM, I, page 96.
12. ACIM, I, page 503.

Other Materials
by Tara Singh

BOOKS

Awakening A Child From Within
Commentaries On A Course In Miracles
How To Learn From A Course In Miracles
"Nothing Real Can Be Threatened"
Dialogues On A Course In Miracles
How To Raise A Child Of God
A Course In Miracles – A Gift For All Mankind
The Voice That Precedes Thought
"Love Holds No Grievances" – The Ending Of Attack
Jesus And The Blind Man – Commentaries on St. John,
Chapter IX
Letters From Mexico
The Present Heals

AUDIO CASSETTE TAPES

Service – Finding Something Of Your Own To Give
Keep The Bowl Empty
Awakening The Light Of The Mind
True Meditation – A Practical Approach
"In God We Trust"
Conflict Ends With Me
What Is A Course In Miracles?
A Course In Miracles Explorations

"What Is The Christ?"
"Creation's Gentleness Is All I See"
Undoing Self-Deception
All Relationships Must End In Love
Is It Possible To Rest The Brain?
Discovering Your Life's Work
The Heart Of Forgiveness
Audiotape Collection from The One Year Non-Commercialized
     Retreat: A Serious Study of A Course In Miracles
Audiotape Collection from The Forty Days In The Wilderness
     Retreats, 1989 & 1990
Best of Tara Singh Retreats – 1990

VIDEO CASSETTE TAPES

A Course In Miracles Is Not To Be Learned, But To Be Lived
How To Raise A Child Of God
The Power Of Attention
"There Must Be Another Way"

A free book and tape catalogue
is available upon request from:
LIFE ACTION PRESS
P.O. Box 48932
Los Angeles, California 90048
213/933-5591

Additional copies of *The Future Of Mankind* by Tara Singh may be obtained by sending a check, money order, Mastercard or Visa number and expiration date to:

LIFE ACTION PRESS
PO Box 48932
Los Angeles, CA 90048
1/800/367-2246

Softcover $12.95
(plus $3.00 shipping/handling)

A Course In Miracles may be purchased from Life Action Press:

Three volume, hardbound ed. $40.00
(plus $4.00 shipping/handling)

Combined, softcover edition $25.00
(plus $4.00 shipping/handling)

California residents please add 8.25% sales tax.

Thank you.

Cover Art: Clio Dixon
Typesetting: The Art Director, Los Angeles, CA
Printing/binding: McNaughton & Gunn, Inc., Saline, MI
Type: Bookman
Paper: 55lb Glatfelter natural (acid free)